THE CORPORATE CURE

THE CORPORATE CURE

A LEADERSHIP FRAMEWORK TO DIAGNOSE, HEAL, AND TRANSFORM YOUR ORGANIZATION

CHRIS TAYLOR

RESULTS FASTER!
PUBLISHING

The Corporate Cure: A Leadership Framework to Diagnose, Heal, and Transform Your Organization

Published by *RESULTS Faster!* Publishing in Flower Mound, TX

Printed in the United States of America

CONTENTS

DEDICATION

This book is dedicated first and foremost to my mother, Jean Taylor.

As a single mother raising four boys, she taught me lessons that shaped not only my life, but the foundation of everything in this book. She taught me the value of determination, hard work, gratitude, faith, and the importance of finding good in all things and in all people. She believed deeply in the power of prayer, continual learning, and the blessings that come through family and service to others.

My mother never stopped learning, growing, or giving. Her love of education and personal growth inspired me to write and to continue searching for ways to help others improve their lives and organizations. My only regret is that I did not finish this book earlier so she could have read it herself. I hope these pages reflect the values she worked so hard to instill in me.

To my wife, Elise Taylor—thank you for being an example of selfless love and service every single day. I have never met anyone more willing to help others, including complete strangers, than you. Your compassion, kindness, and generosity constantly remind me what truly matters most in life. Thank you for supporting me through the long hours, late nights, and endless ideas that eventually became this book. Without your encouragement and belief in me, *The Corporate Cure* would still be little more than notes and outlines.

And finally, to my children and grandchildren—thank you for bringing so much joy, purpose, and energy into my life. You are a constant reminder of why leadership matters, why culture matters, and why building something meaningful matters. You inspire me to continue learning, growing, serving, and doing my small part to help make this world a little better than I found it.

This book is because of all of you.

FOREWORD

Several years back, I met Chris and was immediately struck by his energy and devotion to helping people think at a higher level. Over time, we've developed a wonderful relationship. I wanted to take a few moments in this foreword to introduce you to the powerful book you're about to read, digest, and potentially use to change the way you think. I saw firsthand that Chris doesn't just talk about leadership, growth, and performance. He lives it. He challenges leaders to look beyond the surface, to move past the noise, and to focus on what truly drives results.

That's exactly what you're about to experience in *The Corporate Cure.*

We are operating in a time where organizations are moving fast—but not always forward. Leaders are busy, teams are stretched, and many are addressing symptoms rather than solving root problems. The result is frustration, inefficiency, and missed potential.

Chris brings a different approach.

This book introduces a powerful framework—C.U.R.E.S.: Clarity, Unity, Readiness, Execution, and Sustainability—that gives leaders a way to step back, assess honestly, and move forward with purpose. It's not complicated, but it is disciplined. And when applied correctly, it can transform how organizations think, operate, and perform.

What I appreciate most about Chris's work is that it is grounded in real-world application. He has spent years working alongside leadership teams, helping them simplify complexity, align around what matters, and execute at a higher level. That experience shows up on every page.

As you read this book, you're going to gain more than insight.

You're going to gain a way to think differently about your organization.

You're going to gain clarity around where breakdowns are actually happening.

You're going to gain practical tools to improve alignment, strengthen execution, and build systems that sustain performance over time.

Most importantly, you're going to be challenged to elevate your expectations of yourself, your team, and your organization.

The leaders who win in today's environment are not the ones who do more. They are the ones who think better, align faster, and execute with precision.

The Corporate Cure will help you do exactly that.

Take the time to absorb it. Reflect on it. Most importantly, apply it.

Because the value of this book isn't in reading it.
The value is in what you do with it.

— Tony Jeary

The RESULTS Guy™
Coach to the World's Top CEOs
Author of the international bestseller, *RESULTS Faster!*

INTRODUCTION

WHY *THE CORPORATE CURE?*

When most people hear the word cure, they think of something powerful.

Relief
Healing
Restoration
A second chance

A cure represents the moment everything begins to change. The point where what was once broken starts to be made whole again. It is not about managing symptoms. It is about eliminating the root cause. It is about restoring health so something can grow, thrive, and endure.

That same concept applies to organizations. Every company, no matter how successful it appears on the surface, eventually faces internal problems that threaten its health. Sometimes those problems are small and can be removed quickly. Sometimes they spread slowly through departments, culture, or leadership. And sometimes they grow unnoticed until they begin affecting the entire organization.

When that happens, leaders have two choices.

Ignore the problem and hope it resolves itself—or confront it and cure it.

The Corporate Cure is about choosing to cure it.

It is about identifying the root issues that are quietly destroying performance and systematically restoring the health of the organization.

Not temporarily.
Not superficially.
But fundamentally.

Because when you cure the root issues:

- **Clarity** replaces confusion.
- **Unity** replaces friction.
- **Readiness** replaces chaos.
- **Execution** replaces intention.
- **Sustainability** replaces short-term wins.

This is the foundation of the **C.U.R.E.S. Framework**. But before we dive into that framework, I want to share the story that inspired it. Because for me, this didn't start in a boardroom. It started with my mom.

I was raised by an incredible single mother. My father was killed in a car accident when I was only seven months old. That left my mom,

Jean Sexsmith Taylor, with the responsibility of raising four young boys on her own. And she did it with a level of strength and grace that still amazes me today.

The only picture with me and my dad.
This was not too long before the accident.

To me, she hung the moon and the stars. She worked full time while raising four boys. She never complained. She never slowed down. She simply showed up every single day and gave everything she had to the people around her.

She was the biggest Los Angeles Dodgers fan you could imagine, loved Karl Malone and John Stockton, and was an avid supporter of the

BYU Cougars. She attended every band concert, every sporting event, and every milestone in our lives.

To us, she wasn't just a mom. She was Supermom. But what made her truly extraordinary wasn't just what she did; it was how she made people feel.

Jean had a rare gift. Whenever you spent time with her, you left better than when you arrived. Jean had a gift for making people feel valued. She never judged anyone. She never raised her voice. If someone needed help, she would give the shirt off her back without hesitation. She invested in people. She built confidence. She created clarity. She brought unity. Long before I ever had language for it, she was living the principles I would later define.

She believed deeply in education and spent her life teaching.

My mom in Nepal teaching orphans. Kids and teaching, two of her favorite things.

She taught high school English at American Fork High School, worked with the Brigham Young University cheerleaders and student body officers, and later earned both a master's degree and a PhD in Educational Psychology.

But her influence extended far beyond the classroom.

My mom had a way of investing in people. You always left with a positive return on investment.

She loved being a mom, but becoming a grandmother might have been her favorite role of all. She had fifteen grandchildren, and she treated every moment with them like it was an adventure.

She loved building sandcastles at the beach.

She loved getting splashed by waves while laughing with the grandkids.

She loved taking them on what she called "grand adventures," often inspired by her love of Winnie the Pooh.

Jean believed life was meant to be lived fully and shared generously.

And she did exactly that.

When I was still a young boy, my mom came home one day with news that changed everything. Doctors had discovered melanoma on her back. Fortunately, it was caught early. The cancer was localized and surgically removed before it could spread.

She healed.
She moved forward.
Life continued.

Years later, another moment arrived that I will never forget.

I came home from school and saw my mom sitting quietly in the kitchen. Something felt different.

She asked me to sit down.

The doctors had discovered a lump in her breast.

The biopsy confirmed it was cancer.

Surgery followed, and the doctors were confident they had removed the entire tumor. To ensure nothing remained, they recommended radiation treatment around the area.

Once again, she fought.
Once again—she healed.

Soon she was back to her routine.

Waking up at 4:00 a.m. to swim lap after lap at the gym, working full time, supporting her family, and continuing to positively impact everyone around her.

Life was full.

The family continued to grow and we continued to be blessed.

And for years, everything was going great and seemed normal again.

Then came the summer of 2009.

Our family was gathered in Scottsdale, Arizona, attending a family reunion. These events were some of my mom's favorite moments in life.

She loved building memories.

She was always filming our family gatherings so we could relive them later during our Monday night family home evenings.

But during that reunion, I noticed something.

Something wasn't quite right.

Because she was normally so joyful and energetic, it was easy to notice even the smallest shift.

A few days after we returned home to Utah, she asked me to come over to her house.

Once again, she sat me down. The cancer had come back.

This time it was different.

It had spread throughout her body.

The doctors told us they weren't sure she would make it to the end of the month. This time, surgery wasn't enough. Radiation alone wasn't enough. They needed something more aggressive. They began treatment. And true to who she was—she fought.

She didn't stop living.
She didn't stop loving.
She didn't stop building memories.

And because of that fight, something incredible happened.

We made it to Christmas 2009.

A Christmas we were never supposed to have.

One day in early 2010, my mom and I sat together laughing as she told stories about her life.

She talked about her early days in Van Nuys, California, when she was newly married with one child and no idea what the future would hold.

She reflected on everything she had experienced:

Raising four boys on her own.
Becoming a grandmother to fifteen grandchildren.
Earning advanced degrees.
Serving around the world.
Teaching, mentoring, and lifting others.

She had lived a life of impact.

As spring turned to May, her spirit remained strong even as her body weakened.

Our family gathered around her.

We sang.
We laughed.
We remembered.

And on May 25, 2010, something remarkable happened.

It snowed.

In Utah, snowfall at the end of May is incredibly rare. But my mom loved snow. To her, it represented peace and purity. As we sat together, watching the snow fall outside the window, singing as a family, she quietly closed her eyes for the final time.

Peacefully. Surrounded by love.

Some people hear that story and see only tragedy. But that's not what I see. Because every time the cancer appeared, it was met with action.

When it was small, it was removed.

When it required more, it was treated.

When it spread, it was fought aggressively.

And because of that, we got more time. Twenty-one more years. More than 184,000 additional hours. Hours where she continued to teach, love, mentor, and influence thousands of people. Treatment didn't just extend her life. **It extended her impact.**

That is the lesson. Not just fighting problems. But restoring health so something meaningful can continue to grow. That is what a cure does.

Organizations are not that different from the human body. Over time, issues develop:

- Misalignment
- Broken processes
- Fear-driven leadership
- Lack of accountability
- Cultural decay

Sometimes those issues are small. Sometimes they spread quietly. And sometimes they go unnoticed until they threaten everything. The worst possible response is not aggressive action. The worst response is doing nothing.

Through more than 30 years of leadership experience, I have seen both outcomes. I have seen organizations ignore problems—and slowly decline. And I have seen leaders confront those problems—and completely transform their organizations. Because when organizations are cured:

- people align;
- teams accelerate;
- leaders execute;
- culture strengthens; and
- results sustain.

That is what *The Corporate Cure* is about.

Not just fixing problems. But restoring organizational health at the root level. So growth is not just achieved—it is sustained.

This book exists to help leaders move beyond managing symptoms—and start curing what's actually holding their organization back. Because success isn't just about growth. It's about building something healthy enough to sustain it. Something strong enough to endure it. And something meaningful enough to leave a lasting impact.

Just like my mom did.

CHAPTER 1

THE SILENT SPREAD

Why Organizations Don't See It—Until It's Too Late

THE HIDDEN NATURE OF THE PROBLEM

There is a dangerous assumption that exists inside almost every organization: If something were really wrong, we would know.

It's a comforting belief. It's also completely false. Because the most dangerous problems in an organization are not the loud ones. They're the silent ones.

They don't show up in dramatic ways. They don't announce themselves in executive meetings. They don't immediately disrupt performance.

Instead, they spread quietly beneath the surface—reshaping behavior, distorting perception, and weakening the system over time.

As Peter Drucker once said, "The greatest danger in times of turbulence is not the turbulence; it is to act with yesterday's logic."

Most organizations are not failing because they ignore problems. They are failing because they don't see them.

Most leaders believe they have a clear view of their organization. They sit in executive meetings. They review dashboards. They hear updates from their teams. From their vantage point, everything appears... reasonable. Not perfect. But manageable.

Growth may be slower than expected. Margins may be tighter than desired. Turnover may be slightly higher than they would like. But nothing screams, "We have cancer." And that's exactly the problem.

Every organization, no matter how sophisticated, operates with *Blind Spots*. These are not failures of intelligence. They are failures of perception. This concept, coined by my friend Tony Jeary, explains that *Blind Spots* are the hidden gaps between what leaders believe is happening in their organization and what is actually being experienced by their teams. They are created by limited perspective, filtered information, and organizational dynamics that soften or hide problems. These *Blind Spots* show up as disconnects (clear strategy vs. confused execution, perceived alignment vs. siloed teams) and are especially dangerous because they prevent leaders from seeing the very issues they are responsible for solving. As a result, problems go undetected, drift sets in, and performance declines over time, making *Blind Spots* one of the primary root causes of organizational dysfunction. Research consistently shows that a significant percentage of leaders operate with behavioral *Blind Spots* that directly impact performance. Even more concerning, leaders are often far better at recognizing problems in others than they are at identifying those same issues in themselves.

This creates a dangerous gap:

- Leaders believe they are clear; teams experience confusion.
- Leaders believe they are aligned; teams feel friction.
- Leaders believe communication is strong; teams stay silent.

That gap is where organizational cancer begins. Here's the part most leaders don't want to admit: Organizations are wired to hide their own problems. When early-warning signs appear, they are often softened, explained away, or reinterpreted in a more favorable light.

- Problems get rationalized.
- Data gets interpreted optimistically.
- Failures get blamed on external factors.
- Warning signs get dismissed.

The organization creates a narrative that says, "We're fine. We just need to push a little harder." And in doing so, it delays the moment of truth. One of the most dangerous signals in any organization is not conflict. It's silence. In many companies, employees see problems long before leadership does. But they don't speak up. Because silence feels safer.

There is a well-documented phenomenon known as "employee silence," where individuals withhold information that could improve the organization. This behavior becomes even more pronounced in environments where blame exists or where speaking up carries risk.

Leadership assumes, "Everything must be working." Meanwhile, under the surface, everything is spreading.

I saw this firsthand in an organization I worked with. In addition to having a strong blame culture, there was a noticeable lack of trust. People were hesitant to speak openly, especially when it came to leadership decisions or organizational issues. In an effort to measure engagement, the organization invested heavily in an "anonymous" employee satisfaction survey.

The results came back overwhelmingly positive. Leadership celebrated. They believed the organization was healthy. They believed employees were engaged and satisfied. But the results were a false positive.

Employees didn't trust that the survey was truly anonymous. They feared that honest responses, especially negative ones, could be traced back to them. And in an environment where fear existed, that risk felt too great. So instead of sharing the truth, they protected themselves.

They filled out the survey with high scores. They gave leadership what they wanted to see. But the real conversations didn't disappear. They just moved.

They showed up:

- around the water cooler;
- in private text messages; and
- during side conversations on company calls.

Frustration grew. Trust declined. Strong performers left. Those who remained often operated at a minimal level—just enough to avoid attention. On the surface, everything looked healthy. Underneath, the cancer was spreading.

Another reason organizations miss problems is because they normalize dysfunction. What starts as a small inefficiency becomes "just how we operate." What starts as misalignment becomes "part of our culture." What starts as poor technology utilization becomes "the system we have."

Over time, the abnormal becomes normal. And once that happens, the organization loses its ability to diagnose itself.

Modern organizations are incredibly complex. Multiple systems. Multiple teams. Multiple layers of leadership. That complexity creates the perfect environment for problems to hide.

Leaders often focus on what they can see—reports, metrics, historical data—while missing the emerging issues created by how systems interact with one another.

In other words: They are looking at what they understand instead of what is actually happening.

Most organizations don't fail because they ignore problems.

They fail because:

- they don't see them, or
- they see symptoms and misdiagnose the cause.

I've seen this play out repeatedly across industries.

Organizations invest millions into technology, processes, and people. On paper, everything looks right:

- Systems are implemented.
- Workflows are built.
- Reports are available.

But performance doesn't improve.

So leadership looks for explanations:

- "The staff needs more training."
- "The market is tough."
- "Reimbursement is the issue."

Instead of asking the harder question, "What are we not seeing?"

Because that question requires something most organizations avoid—honest self-diagnosis. And once you accept that the problem is often invisible, you're forced to confront the next reality: Are you looking at symptoms, or are you actually identifying the disease?

SYMPTOMS VS. ROOT CAUSES

This section reveals something even more dangerous than organizations not seeing the problem: Even when they do see something wrong, they misdiagnose it.

In medicine, a fever is not the disease. It's a signal. You can reduce the fever temporarily; but if you never address the underlying infection, the patient gets worse. The same is true in business.

Organizations focus on symptoms because they are:

- visible;
- measurable;
- urgent; and
- pressure-filled.

So leaders react. They launch initiatives. They buy technology. They restructure teams. They increase oversight. And for a short time, things appear to improve.

Until they don't.

The Organizational Treatment Loop:

1. A symptom appears
2. Leadership reacts quickly
3. A surface-level fix is implemented
4. Short-term improvement occurs
5. The problem returns—often worse

This cycle is exhausting, and it's incredibly common. Root causes don't show up clearly. They don't sit on dashboards. They don't announce themselves in meetings. They exist underneath the surface—in how the organization actually operates.

They look like:

- lack of clarity in priorities;
- misaligned leadership incentives;
- teams working in silos;
- underutilized technology;
- lack of readiness for change;
- inconsistent execution discipline;
- short-term thinking overriding sustainability; and/or
- lack of trust in management.

The Corporate Cure is built on a simple but powerful shift:

Stop treating what you see.
Start diagnosing what's causing it.

Because once you identify the true root cause, the solution becomes clear. And that leads to the next reality: Misdiagnosis isn't just inefficient. It's expensive.

THE COST OF LATE DETECTION

Cancer is most dangerous when it's found too late. Not because it suddenly became aggressive, but because it was spreading long before anyone noticed. The same is true in organizations.

Most leaders believe: "We'll fix it when it becomes a real problem."

But by the time a problem is visible, it's already been there for months—or even years. And during that time, it's been spreading. Late detection doesn't show up as one big event. It shows up as compounding losses. And the most dangerous cost of all? Lost time. Time when the organization could have been growing, improving, and aligning. Time you don't get back.

WHERE IT HIDES

Organizational cancer doesn't show up randomly. It follows patterns.

Most organizations try to solve problems in isolation:

- Sales is underperforming.
- Operations is behind.

- Technology isn't working.
- Culture feels off.

But what if those aren't separate problems? What if they're all symptoms of the same underlying condition?

High-performing organizations understand something critical:

If you solve the pattern, you eliminate multiple problems at once.

The Silent Spread is not about fear. It's about awareness.

Late detection doesn't show up as one big event. It shows up as compounding losses. And the most dangerous cost of all? Lost time.

Because once you understand:

- why organizations don't see the problem;
- how they misdiagnose it;
- the cost of waiting; and
- where it hides,

you're no longer guessing. You're ready to diagnose.

And that leads to the next step: If organizational cancer exists, how do you identify it early?

Because the organizations that win are not the ones that avoid problems.

They are the ones that detect them first.

If you solve the pattern, you eliminate multiple problems at once.

VERY IMPORTANT POINTS

1. The most dangerous organizational problems are often invisible at first. Leaders may believe everything is manageable because dashboards, meetings, and reports look reasonable, while deeper issues spread quietly beneath the surface.
2. *Blind Spots* create the gap where organizational cancer begins. Leaders may believe they are clear, aligned, and communicating well, while teams experience confusion, friction, and silence.
3. Treating symptoms instead of root causes keeps organizations trapped in a costly cycle. Quick fixes may create short-term improvement; but if the underlying issues remain undiagnosed, the problem returns—often worse.
4. Early detection is a competitive advantage. High-performing organizations do not avoid problems altogether; they identify hidden patterns early, diagnose the real issue, and solve root causes instead of reacting to symptoms.

CHAPTER 2

IDENTIFYING ORGANIZATIONAL CANCER

Once you accept that the most dangerous problems in an organization often go unseen, the next question becomes unavoidable: **How do you actually identify them before it's too late?**

The organizations that win are not the ones that avoid problems. They are the ones that detect them early.

In medicine, early detection saves lives.

In business, it saves everything that matters:

- Revenue
- Talent
- Culture
- Momentum

And yet, most organizations do not have a system for early detection.

Instead, they rely on instinct. They wait for lagging metrics. They react to escalated issues. They respond only when something becomes obvious.

But high-performing organizations operate differently. They understand a fundamental truth: Every major failure starts as a small, detectable signal.

Organizational cancer does not appear overnight. It whispers first.

The problem is that most leaders are listening for alarms—not whispers.

Early warning indicators are rarely dramatic. They are subtle, easy to overlook, and even easier to rationalize. They show up in small shifts that, on their own, do not seem urgent.

They look like:

- a team that used to move fast now hesitates;
- meetings that feel slightly more tense than before;
- a process that takes a little longer each month;
- a key employee who becomes disengaged; and
- a system that people "work around" instead of use.

Individually, none of these raise immediate concern.

But together, they form a pattern.

The reason these signals are missed is not because leaders are careless. It's because early indicators are labeled as "normal growing pains," "temporary issues," or "market conditions." They are explained away instead of explored.

But research in organizational behavior consistently shows that small inefficiencies, when repeated over time, compound into significant performance loss.

Great leaders don't wait for certainty. They investigate signals.

They ask better questions:

- "Why is this happening now?"
- "Where else is this showing up?"
- "What's changing beneath the surface?"

Because they understand something most organizations miss: If you wait until it's obvious, you're already late.

Most organizations do not collapse. They drift.

Drift does not look like failure. It does not feel like crisis. It shows up as gradual decline—small, incremental changes that seem manageable in isolation but become dangerous in aggregate.

Growth slows. Margins tighten. Execution becomes inconsistent. Accountability weakens.

Each shift is small enough to ignore.

Together, they tell a very different story.

Humans are wired to notice sharp changes, not gradual ones. This is why drift is so dangerous.

There is a concept known as "normalization of deviance," widely studied in organizational and safety research. It describes how small deviations from optimal performance become accepted over time because they do not immediately result in failure.

Until they do.

Here's an example that I've seen happen in real time. A retail company began to see small, seemingly unrelated issues:

- Slight dips in customer satisfaction
- Slight increases in product returns
- Slight delays in fulfillment

If you wait until it's obvious, you're already late.

No single issue triggered alarm. But over eighteen months, the pattern became clear: Customer retention dropped significantly. Brand perception declined. Revenue flattened. There was no sudden crisis. There was drift.

THE 7 ORGANIZATIONAL CANCERS

Through years of consulting, leadership, and real-world experience, I began to see patterns emerge. Different companies. Different industries. Same problems. These seven cancers show up again and again.

What follows is a brief synopsis of the most common patterns of organizational breakdown—what we refer to as "organizational cancers." These are not isolated issues or one-off problems. They are recurring,

ORGANIZATIONAL CANCER TYPES

DIAGNOSIS ⟶ SEVERITY ⟶ TREATMENT

CANCER TYPE	WHAT IT LOOKS LIKE	EFFECTS	BREAKS IN C.U.R.E.S. / BROT	SEVERITY	TREATMENT (C.U.R.E.S. + BROT)	SIGNATURE LINE
FEAR-BASED LEADERSHIP	Public criticism, intimidation, silence, punishment over learning	Low trust, no innovation, disengagement, minimal effort	BROT (Trust), Unity	HIGH (Fast-Spreading)	• Implement BROT (Build Relationships of Trust) • Create psychological safety • Replace fear with accountability + coaching • Leader behavior reset	*"Fear may drive compliance... but it kills commitment."*
EGO-DRIVEN LEADERSHIP	Leader must be right, no feedback, dismisses input	Poor decisions, talent loss, fragile org, stagnation	Unity, Clarity	HIGH (Leadership-Centric)	• Introduce feedback loops • Use data-driven decision frameworks • Leadership coaching & 360 reviews • Shift from "I" → "We" mindset	*"When ego leads... truth disappears."*
MISALIGNED INCENTIVES	Teams competing, siloed goals, selfish wins rewarded	Internal conflict, poor collaboration, bad outcomes	Unity, Execution	HIGH (Systemic)	• Align compensation with shared outcomes • Create cross-functional KPIs • Reward collaboration • Remove conflicting metrics	*"People don't do what you say... they do what you reward."*
OVERCOMPLEXITY CANCER	Too many tools, priorities, processes, constant confusion	Slow execution, burnout, inefficiency	Clarity, Execution	MEDIUM (Creeping Cancer)	• Reduce to 3–5 priorities max • Simplify workflows • Eliminate redundant tools • Standardize processes	*"Complexity is the silent killer of execution."*
LACK OF HONEST SELF-ASSESSMENT	Ignoring problems, avoiding data, leadership bias	Late detection, compounding issues, missed opportunities	Clarity, Readiness	HIGH (Hidden Cancer)	• Implement diagnostic scorecards • Use data dashboards • Conduct regular business reviews • Encourage truth over comfort	*"You can't cure what you refuse to diagnose."*
TECHNOLOGY ILLUSION CANCER	Buying tools w/o adoption, relying on tech to fix problems	Wasted spend, frustration, no ROI	Readiness, Execution	MEDIUM (Expensive Cancer)	• Focus on adoption, not purchase • Train teams properly • Align tech with workflows • Track usage + ROI	*"Technology doesn't fix broken systems... it exposes them."*
INITIATIVE OVERLOAD / CHANGE SATURATION	Too many initiatives, constant change, no prioritization	Burnout, failed initiatives, lack of progress	Readiness, Sustainability	HIGH (Burnout Accelerator)	• Limit active initiatives • Sequence change intentionally • Build change capacity planning • Reinforce and sustain before adding new	*"When everything is a priority... nothing gets done."*

systemic patterns that appear across industries, leadership teams, and operating models. While they may look different on the surface, they share a common trait: They develop quietly, spread over time, and erode performance long before they are fully recognized.

Each synopsis is designed to help you quickly identify the signals, understand the underlying impact, and recognize where these patterns may exist within your own organization. The goal is not simply awareness, but clarity—the ability to name what you're actually dealing with. Because once you can clearly identify the problem, you are no longer reacting to symptoms. You are in a position to diagnose accurately, act intentionally, and begin restoring the system that drives performance.

For a deeper exploration of each of these patterns, including real-world examples and treatment approaches, refer to the Appendix.

1. Fear-Based Leadership

When accountability becomes intimidation

Fear may create short-term compliance, but it destroys long-term performance. Fear-based leadership is one of the most visible—and most misunderstood—forms of organizational breakdown.

There is a common assumption: "If people feel pressure, they'll perform better."

That belief has damaged more organizations than it has improved.

The reality is very different.

Research consistently shows that environments driven by fear reduce psychological safety, limit communication, and suppress innovation. What looks like discipline on the surface is often dysfunction underneath.

The problem is rarely accountability. It is how accountability is delivered.

What it looks like:

- Public pressure and humiliation
- Silence in meetings
- Avoidance of risk

Impact:

- Trust collapses
- Innovation disappears
- Engagement declines

Fear may drive compliance, but it kills commitment.

2. Ego-Driven Leadership

When the leader becomes the limiting factor

Leaders say they want feedback, but only accept what aligns with their thinking.

There is a common assumption: Strong leaders have strong opinions.

That belief often goes unchecked.

The reality is very different.

Research consistently shows that high-performing leaders combine confidence with humility. When ego replaces humility, decision-making narrows, feedback disappears, and *Blind Spots* grow.

The problem is rarely confidence. It is the inability to separate identity from ideas. These are not communication problems. They are truth problems.

I once worked with a leadership team that believed they were highly collaborative. Meetings were open, ideas were shared—but only the leader's perspective moved forward. Over time, behavior changed. People stopped offering real input. Alignment appeared strong, but it was artificial.

The organization didn't become aligned. It became compliant.

*When ego leads,
truth disappears.*

What it looks like:

- Ideas dismissed or minimized
- Public criticism of input
- "Yes-men" culture

Impact:

- Innovation stalls
- Talent leaves
- Poor decisions go unchallenged

When ego leads, truth disappears.

3. Misaligned Incentives

When the system rewards the wrong behavior

People don't do what you say. They do what you reward. There is a common assumption: If we set goals and compensation, performance will follow.

That belief is often incomplete.

The reality is very different.

Incentives shape behavior more than strategy, culture, or communication. When incentives are misaligned, they don't just fail to drive performance—they actively distort it.

You can't out-coach a broken incentive system.

The problem is rarely effort. It is what the system is encouraging people to do. I once worked with a sales organization where compensation was tied only to closed deals, despite a long sales cycle and limited pipeline. The result was predictable. Activity slowed, morale dropped, and growth stalled—not because of the people, but because the system failed to reward the behaviors needed to succeed.

What it looks like:

- Teams competing internally
- Short-term wins over long-term value

- Conflicting goals

Impact:

- Broken collaboration
- Poor customer outcomes
- Organizational friction

4. Overcomplexity

When more becomes the enemy of better

What starts as improvement becomes friction.

There is a common assumption: If we add more structure, tools, or processes, performance will improve.

That belief often backfires.

The reality is very different.

As organizations grow, layers are added—systems, workflows, priorities—all intended to improve outcomes. But over time, those layers begin to slow execution, reduce clarity, and create confusion.

What it looks like:

- Too many tools, processes, and priorities
- Confusion across teams
- Systems that are hard to use

Impact:

- Slow execution
- Burnout

- Lost efficiency

Complexity is the silent killer of execution.

5. Lack of Honest Self-Assessment

When organizations stop telling themselves the truth

There is a common assumption: If something were really wrong, we would know.

That belief is comforting—and completely false.

Organizations are wired to protect themselves from uncomfortable truths. Data gets interpreted optimistically. Problems get explained away. Early warning signs are dismissed as temporary issues instead of investigated as signals.

The problem is rarely a lack of information. It is a lack of honest interpretation.

What it looks like:

- Avoidance of hard questions
- Assumptions instead of data
- Delayed recognition of problems

Impact:

- Late problem detection
- Leadership *Blind Spots*
- False confidence

You can't cure what you refuse to diagnose.

6. Technology Illusion

When tools are mistaken for solutions

Technology doesn't fix problems; it amplifies them. Technology is one of the most visible—and most misunderstood—areas of organizational cancer.

There is a common assumption: If the technology isn't working, we need better technology.

That belief has cost organizations billions.

The reality is very different.

Technology doesn't fix broken systems; it exposes them.

Studies consistently show that a large percentage of digital transformation initiatives fail to deliver expected results—not because of the technology itself, but because of organizational issues surrounding it.

The problem is rarely the tool. It is the system around it.

Technology underperformance does not always announce itself loudly. It shows up in subtle but consistent patterns:

- Low adoption rates
- Teams relying on manual workarounds

- Inconsistent or unreliable data
- Reports that exist but are never used
- Features that were purchased but never implemented

These are not technology problems. They are organizational problems.

I once witnessed a logistics company invest heavily in a new operations platform. The expectation was improved efficiency, better visibility, and stronger performance.

Six months later, the reality looked very different:

- Only 40 percent of the platform's features were being used
- Teams had reverted to spreadsheets
- Leadership questioned the return on investment

The platform had not failed. The organization had failed to align around it.

What it looks like:

- Heavy investment in tools
- Poor adoption
- Misaligned workflows

Impact:

- Low ROI
- Frustration
- Bad data driving bad decisions

Technology doesn't fix broken systems; it exposes them.

7. Initiative Overload/Change Saturation

When everything is important, and nothing gets done

More initiatives do not equal more progress. There is a common assumption: If we do more, we'll achieve more.

That belief creates the opposite effect.

The reality is very different.

When organizations launch too many initiatives at once, focus disappears. Teams become overwhelmed. Priorities compete. Execution suffers—not because people aren't working hard, but because they are pulled in too many directions.

The problem is rarely effort. It is lack of focus and capacity.

What it looks like:

- Too many priorities
- Constant change
- Lack of focus

Impact:

- Burnout
- Slow execution
- Incomplete initiatives

When everything is a priority, nothing gets done.

HOW THE CANCERS CONNECT

These cancers rarely exist in isolation. They feed each other.

- Fear kills trust → Unity breaks
- Ego blocks truth → Clarity distorts
- Misaligned incentives → Execution fractures
- Overcomplexity → Slows everything
- Lack of assessment → Problems go unseen
- Technology illusion → Multiplies inefficiency
- Initiative overload → Prevents sustainability

You're rarely dealing with one problem—you're often dealing with a system of problems.

When everything is a priority, nothing gets done.

THE TREATMENT: C.U.R.E.S. + BROT

You don't fight these cancers individually. You treat the system.

C.U.R.E.S.

- **Clarity** → Define direction
- **Unity** → Align people

- **Readiness** → Prepare for growth
- **Execution** → Deliver results
- **Sustainability** → Make it last

BROT (Build Relationships of Trust)

Trust is the multiplier.

Without it:

- Unity fails
- Execution weakens
- Sustainability disappears

Trust is the sunlight that allows everything else to grow.

VERY IMPORTANT POINTS

1. Every major failure starts as a small, detectable signal. Organizational cancer rarely appears suddenly; it begins as subtle shifts like hesitation, tension, delays, disengagement, or workarounds.
2. Leaders must learn to listen for whispers, not just alarms. Early warning signs are often rationalized as growing pains, temporary issues, or market conditions; but great leaders investigate signals before they become obvious.
3. Organizational drift is dangerous because it feels manageable. Small declines in growth, margins, execution, and accountability may seem minor in isolation; but together they reveal a deeper pattern of decline.
4. The seven organizational cancers are systemic patterns, not isolated problems. Fear-based leadership, ego-driven leadership, misaligned incentives, overcomplexity, lack of honest self-assessment, technology illusion, and initiative overload often feed each other and must be treated as a system.

CHAPTER 3

THE FALSE CURE PROBLEM

Why Most Organizations Try to Fix the Right Problems the Wrong Way

By now, the patterns are becoming clear.

You understand that problems don't appear overnight. You recognize that symptoms are not the same as root causes. You've seen how delays allow issues to spread quietly beneath the surface.

So logically, once organizations recognize that something is wrong, they should be able to fix it. But they don't. At least, not effectively.

Most organizations are not failing because they ignore problems. They are failing because they are applying the wrong cures to the right diagnoses. And in many cases, those cures make things worse.

This is where the danger compounds. Because once an organization believes it is taking action, it often stops asking whether that action is actually solving the problem.

When pressure rises, organizations don't slow down to diagnose. They speed up. They act. Quick fixes feel productive because they create visible motion. Leaders can point to action. Teams can point to effort. The organization feels like it is responding. But movement is not the same as progress.

Quick fixes often show up in familiar ways:

- Adding more meetings instead of fixing alignment
- Hiring more people instead of fixing process
- Replacing systems instead of fixing usage
- Increasing accountability instead of clarifying expectations

Each of these actions may provide temporary relief. They reduce pressure in the moment. They create the appearance of control. But they rarely solve the real issue.

Research on organizational change consistently shows that nearly 70 percent of transformation efforts fail—largely due to lack of proper diagnosis and sustainable execution.

That failure is not due to lack of effort. It is due to misdirected effort.

As Peter Drucker famously said, "There is nothing so useless as doing efficiently that which should not be done at all."

Quick fixes address symptoms. They ignore root causes. They create temporary improvement—and then lead to recurring problems.

FALSE CURE #1: The Consultant Carousel

When Advice Replaces Accountability

One of the most common patterns in struggling organizations is what can best be described as the "consultant carousel."

At first, it looks like progress. A strategy firm is brought in to redefine direction. A culture firm is engaged to improve engagement. A technology firm implements new systems. An operations firm redesigns workflows.

Each brings value. Each delivers insights. Each produces output.

And yet, nothing sticks.

Because each engagement solves a piece of the problem, but not the system itself.

Over time, the organization begins to cycle through solutions without ever resolving the underlying issue. The result is predictable:

- Conflicting frameworks
- Overlapping initiatives
- Leadership confusion
- Team fatigue

For example, I once worked with a mid-market company that cycled through four consulting firms in three years:

- A strategy firm delivered a new plan.
- A culture firm introduced new values.

- A technology firm implemented a new platform.
- An operations firm redesigned processes.

Three years later, the organization faced the same problems. Only now, they described them differently.

"If you don't know what problem you're solving, any solution looks good."
— Clayton Christensen

The root issue was not effort. It was not investment. It was the absence of a unified diagnostic model. There was no system connecting the work.

C.U.R.E.S. Connection

The consultant carousel fails because it lacks three things:

- **Clarity** → No true diagnosis
- **Unity** → No aligned approach
- **Execution** → No follow-through across initiatives

FALSE CURE #2: Technology Overbuying

When Tools Replace Thinking

When organizations don't get the results they expect, they often turn to technology. They assume that better tools will produce better outcomes.

"If we just had the right system…"

"If we upgraded the platform…"

"If we invested in new technology..."

This belief feels logical. But it is often wrong.

Research consistently shows that a significant percentage of technology investments fail to deliver expected ROI—not because of the technology itself, but because of poor adoption, unclear use, and lack of integration.

The issue is not what was purchased. It is how it is used.

Technology overbuying often creates complexity rather than clarity:

- Multiple tools performing similar functions
- Systems that are not integrated
- Teams selecting their own tools independently
- Data that is inconsistent across platforms

I once worked with a professional services firm that had accumulated:

- three project management tools;
- two CRM systems; and
- four reporting platforms.

Leadership believed they had a visibility problem. In reality, they had a clarity and execution problem.

> ***"Technology is best when it brings people together. It fails when it replaces thinking."***
> **— Simon Sinek**

C.U.R.E.S. Connection

Technology overbuying reflects breakdowns in:

- **Clarity** → Why are we using this?

- **Readiness** → Are we prepared?
- **Execution** → Are we using it effectively?

FALSE CURE #3: Initiative Fatigue

When Effort Becomes Exhaustion

This is where organizations begin to wear down. Not because they lack ambition, but because they have too much of it, applied in the wrong way.

When something isn't working, the default response is to launch another initiative. Another program. Another transformation effort. Each one is intended to solve a problem. But collectively, they create overload.

What It Looks Like

- Constant introduction of new initiatives
- Previous initiatives never fully completed
- Teams feeling overwhelmed and disengaged
- Leaders frustrated by lack of progress

One organization I worked with had:

- twelve active "top priorities";
- seven transformation initiatives; and
- five new systems being implemented simultaneously.

The result? Nothing was executed well. Teams were exhausted. Leadership blamed execution. But the real issue was not execution. It was lack of clarity and readiness.

"If everything is a priority, nothing is."
— Stephen Covey

C.U.R.E.S. Connection

Initiative fatigue breaks:

- **Clarity** → Too many priorities
- **Readiness** → Too much change
- **Execution** → Nothing gets completed

FALSE CURE #4: Culture Theater vs. Real Change

When It Looks Like Progress But Isn't

This is one of the most deceptive forms of false cure. Because it looks like progress.

Organizations launch culture initiatives with visible, positive actions:

- New mission statements
- Core values posters
- Team-building events
- Engagement surveys

These efforts are not inherently bad. But on their own, they are insufficient.

Culture is not defined by what you say. It is defined by what you consistently reinforce.

Real change requires:

- alignment of leadership behavior;
- clear accountability systems;
- consistent reinforcement; and
- integration into daily operations.

A company launched a culture transformation initiative that included new values, new messaging, and new branding.

But leadership behavior did not change. Incentives remained the same. Accountability was inconsistent. Within months, nothing had changed.

"Culture eats strategy for breakfast."
— Peter Drucker

C.U.R.E.S. Connection

Culture theater fails because it ignores:

- **Unity** → Alignment of leadership behavior
- **Execution** → Consistent reinforcement
- **Sustainability** → Long-term systems

Bringing It All Together

False cures are dangerous—not because they do nothing, but because they create the illusion that something is being done.

They:

- consume time and resources;
- delay real solutions; and

- erode trust within the organization.

And over time, they make the real problem harder to fix.

The Corporate Cure is built on a fundamentally different philosophy.

You don't treat symptoms.
You don't chase solutions.
You diagnose first.
Then you treat with precision.

Now that we've exposed:

- the silent spread;
- the patterns of dysfunction; and
- the failure of false cures,

we're ready for the most important shift in the book: How do you actually fix it, systematically, sustainably, and at the root?

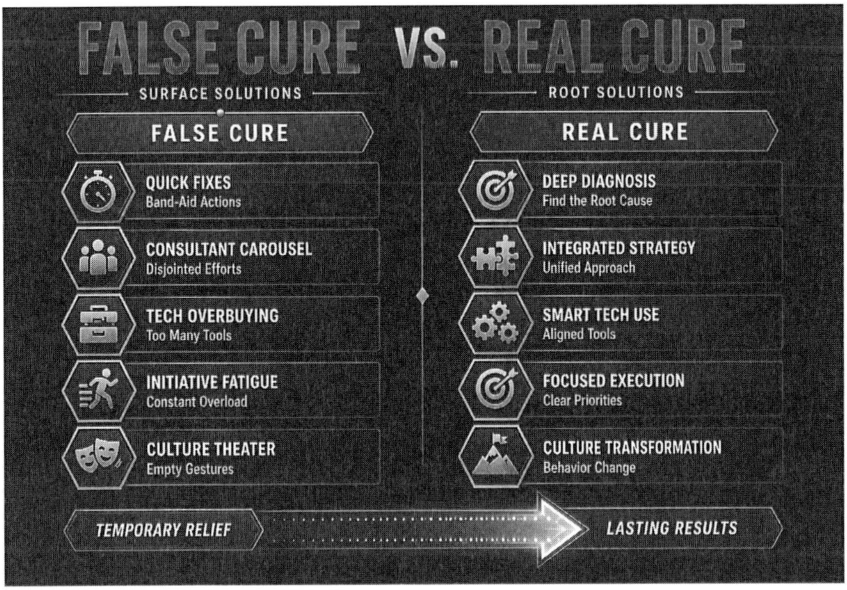

VERY IMPORTANT POINTS

1. Most organizations fail because they apply the wrong cures to the right problems. Once leaders believe they are taking action, they often stop asking whether the action is actually solving the root issue.
2. Quick fixes create motion, but not necessarily progress. More meetings, more hires, new systems, or tighter accountability may reduce pressure temporarily; but they often treat symptoms instead of causes.
3. False cures create the illusion of improvement while delaying real solutions. The consultant carousel, technology overbuying, initiative fatigue, and culture theater can consume time, money, and trust without fixing the underlying system.
4. The real cure begins with diagnosis before action. *The Corporate Cure* is built on a different philosophy: Stop chasing solutions, identify the root cause first, and then treat with precision.

CHAPTER 4

CLARITY

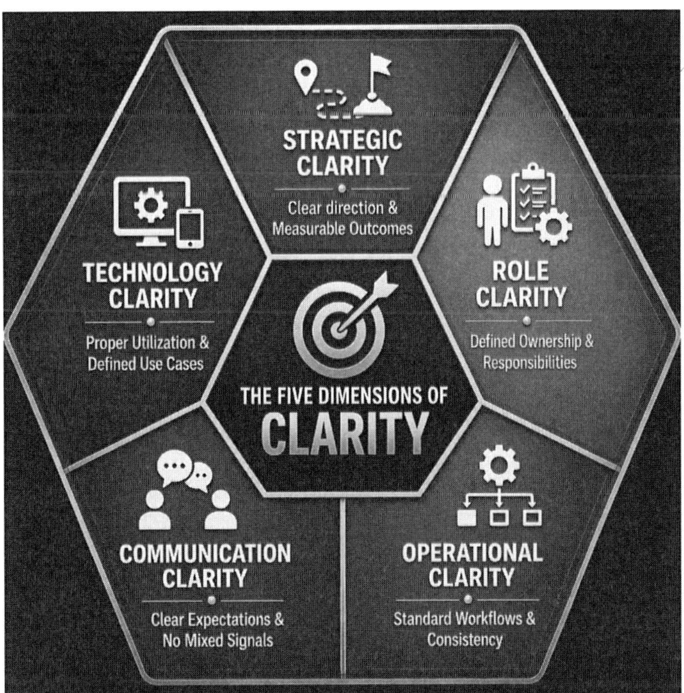

There is a moment every organization eventually experiences. People are working hard, but progress feels slow. Meetings are happening, but decisions don't stick. Strategies are created, but execution feels scattered. From the outside, it looks like an execution problem. But it's not. It's a visibility problem.

Imagine driving seventy miles per hour down the highway. Now imagine doing it in thick fog. The car still works. The road is still there. You are still capable of driving. But everything changes. You slow down. You hesitate. You second-guess. You grip the wheel tighter. Not because you are incapable, but because you cannot see clearly.

This is exactly what happens inside organizations.

When clarity is low, behavior changes in predictable ways:

- Teams hesitate
- Leaders overcorrect

- Employees second-guess
- Execution slows

Organizations don't stall because they lack effort; they stall because they lack clarity.

Clarity is often misunderstood. It is not communication alone. It is not a PowerPoint presentation. It is not a quarterly strategy deck. Clarity exists when people truly understand how to operate.

It means:

- people know what matters most;
- people know what to do;
- people know what success looks like; and
- people know what **not** to focus on.

As Yogi Berra famously said, "If you don't know where you are going, you'll end up someplace else."

Clarity is direction made actionable.

Low clarity does not usually show up as obvious confusion. It shows up as friction.

You begin to see patterns like:

- too many competing priorities;
- constantly shifting direction;
- meetings that end without decisions;
- teams working hard, but on different things; and
- leaders sending mixed messages.

The organization appears busy. But it is not aligned.

I saw a fast-growing SaaS company make the decision to "accelerate growth."

The leadership team launched multiple initiatives at once:

- A new product line
- A new pricing model
- A new sales motion
- A new marketing strategy

Individually, each initiative made sense. But together, they created chaos.

Organizations don't stall because they lack effort; they stall because they lack clarity.

Sales didn't know what to sell. Marketing didn't know what to promote. Product didn't know what to prioritize. Revenue stalled. Not because the strategy was wrong, but because the organization lacked the clarity required to execute it.

Here's another example: In a hospice organization, leadership introduced several important changes:

- A new EMR workflow
- New compliance documentation requirements
- Updated IDG processes

Each of these changes was necessary. But what was missing was clarity.

Leadership did not clearly define:

- what success looked like;
- what mattered most; and
- how teams should prioritize.

The result was predictable. Nurses documented differently. Compliance risk increased. Frustration grew. Leadership blamed execution. But the problem wasn't execution. It was clarity.

Low clarity creates hidden costs that compound over time.

It leads to:

- wasted effort;
- rework;
- frustration;
- burnout; and
- missed opportunities.

As Stephen Covey said, "When everything is a priority, nothing is."

And as leadership expert Brené Brown reinforces, "Clear is kind. Unclear is unkind."

Lack of clarity is not neutral. It is costly.

Clarity in the C.U.R.E.S. Framework

Clarity is the first step in the C.U.R.E.S. Framework for a reason. Because without clarity, nothing else works.

Without clarity:

- unity is impossible;
- readiness is misjudged;
- execution becomes inconsistent; and
- sustainability never takes hold.

You cannot align people to something they do not clearly understand.

Clarity is not a single concept. It is built across five critical areas:

1. Strategic Clarity
Do we know where we are going?

- Clear direction
- Defined priorities
- Measurable outcomes

2. Role Clarity
Do people know what they own?

- Clear responsibilities
- Defined ownership
- Decision rights

3. Operational Clarity
Do we know how work gets done?

- Standard workflows
- Defined processes
- Consistency

4. Communication Clarity
Are messages consistent?

- No mixed signals
- Repetition of priorities
- Clear expectations

5. Technology Clarity
Are tools aligned with purpose?

- Defined use cases
- Proper utilization
- No tool overload

Clarity does not happen by accident. It is created through disciplined leadership decisions. It begins with ruthless prioritization.

Leaders must ask, "What are the top three priorities?"

Everything else becomes secondary.

Success must also be clearly defined. Not vague goals like "Improve performance," but specific outcomes like "Reduce charting time by 30 percent in 90 days."

Competing initiatives must be eliminated. One clear direction will always outperform five competing ones.

And communication must be consistent and repetitive. Leaders must say the same things, over and over again, until there is no ambiguity left.

As Robin Sharma said, "Clarity precedes success."

Clarity is uncomfortable. Because it forces leaders to make hard decisions. To choose. To eliminate. To say no. But without those decisions, everything suffers.

Most organizations struggle with clarity—not because they don't understand its importance, but because they avoid the discipline required to create it.

Clarity → The Bridge to Unity

This is where everything connects. When clarity exists, people understand priorities. Teams move in the same direction. Decisions reinforce each other. That alignment creates something powerful: unity.

Clarity tells people where to go. Unity determines whether they go there together.

Driving in fog slows everything down. Not because the car is broken, but because visibility is limited.

Organizations are no different. If you want your organization to move faster, you don't start by pushing harder. You start by helping people see clearly.

If you want your organization to move faster, you don't push harder. You help people see clearly.

VERY IMPORTANT POINTS

1. Organizations don't stall because they lack effort; they stall because they lack clarity. When visibility is low, teams hesitate, leaders overcorrect, employees second guess, and execution slows.
2. Clarity means people understand how to operate. It is more than communication; it means people know what matters most, what to do, what success looks like, and what not to focus on.
3. Low clarity creates friction that looks like poor execution. Competing priorities, shifting direction, unclear ownership, mixed messages, and disconnected teams often signal a clarity problem—not a people problem.
4. Clarity is the foundation for the rest of C.U.R.E.S. Without clarity, unity is impossible, readiness is misjudged, execution becomes inconsistent, and sustainability never takes hold.

CHAPTER 5

UNITY

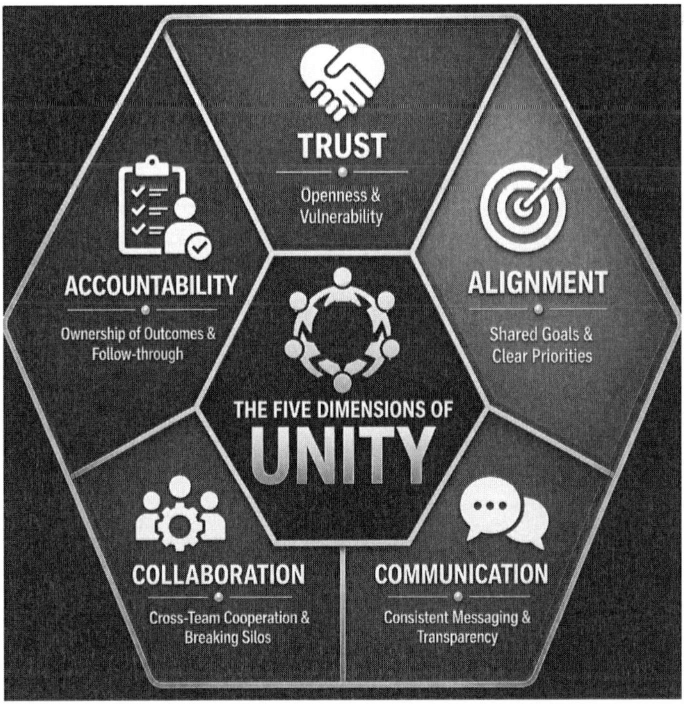

If Clarity defines direction, Unity determines whether the organization actually moves together.

Because no matter how strong your strategy is, no matter how clear your priorities are, if your people are not aligned, your organization will never perform at its full potential.

Clarity tells people where to go. Unity determines whether they go there together.

Unity is often misunderstood. It is not agreement. It is alignment.

It is the difference between people nodding their heads in meetings and people moving in the same direction in execution.

Unity exists when leaders operate from the same priorities, when teams reinforce each other's work instead of competing with it, and when decisions across the organization build on each other rather than contradict.

Most organizations believe they are aligned. But what they actually have is agreement in meetings—and misalignment in execution.

As George Bernard Shaw famously said, "The single biggest problem in communication is the illusion that it has taken place."

Unity is not what is said. It is what is consistently executed.

When Unity breaks down, it rarely announces itself directly. It shows up in patterns.

You begin to see:

- cross-functional friction;
- conflicting priorities;
- duplicated work;

- internal competition; and
- slow decision-making.

Inside the organization, it feels even more fragmented. Sales blames operations. Operations blames leadership. Leadership questions execution.

Everyone is working. But no one is working together.

Misalignment is one of the most expensive problems in business.

Research consistently shows that poor alignment leads to reduced productivity, slower execution, increased turnover, and lost revenue opportunities. But there is an even deeper cost.

It is not just inefficiency. It is energy loss.

When teams are misaligned, effort cancels out effort. Work gets redone. Progress slows. Momentum disappears.

Mark Twain described synergy as the bonus that is achieved when things work together harmoniously.

Without Unity, there is no synergy.

Most leaders assume misalignment is a process problem. It is not. It is a trust problem.

BROT: The Foundation of Unity

Build Relationships of Trust

There is one variable that determines whether an organization thrives or slowly breaks down. It is not strategy. It is not talent. It is not even execution.

It is trust.

In business, trust is often treated like a soft skill—something nice to have, something to include in value statements, something to reference in leadership conversations.

But in reality, trust is the most critical performance driver in any organization.

As Stephen Covey said, "Trust is the glue of life. It's the most essential ingredient in effective communication."

Without trust, communication breaks down. Alignment disappears. Execution slows. Innovation stops.

With trust, everything accelerates.

Trust is the sunlight of an organization. It brings warmth. It creates clarity. It fuels growth.

Without sunlight, nothing grows. Without trust, neither do organizations.

What would the earth be without sunlight? How long would we last without it?

Now ask yourself:

What is a leader without trust? How long will they effectively lead?
What is an organization without trust? How long will it truly last?

Trust is not accidental. It is built.

That is why every leader, every team, and every organization must: **BROT—Build Relationships of Trust.**

Because when you consciously invest in trust, everything changes.

Trust is not a concept. It's a system. And like any system, it must be built intentionally.

Flow of Trust-Building:

1. Lead with Trust → Starts at leadership
2. Listen with Trust → Creates safety
3. Build with Trust → Drives collaboration
4. Reinforce with Trust → Sustains culture

And it loops, because trust is not a one-time action; it's a system.

What Happens When BROT Is Missing

Without trust, behavior shifts in predictable ways. People begin to protect instead of collaborate. Teams compete instead of align. Silence replaces truth. Compliance replaces commitment.

Research from Amy Edmondson on psychological safety reinforces this reality. Teams that lack trust experience lower performance, reduced innovation, and higher error rates.

Without trust:

- innovation drops;
- performance declines; and
- errors increase.

Trust is not a cultural bonus. It is a performance requirement.

Trust is not a concept.

I walked into an organization as the VP of Marketing and Sales. From the outside, the problems looked familiar: Low sales. Weak pipeline. Poor teamwork. No clear direction.

But within the first week, it became clear that these were not the real problems. The real problem was simple: There was no trust.

Teammates did not trust each other. Employees did not trust leadership. Leadership did not trust the organization. And because of that, nothing worked.

The Hidden Cancer: Internal Competition

One of the clearest examples was a behavior known as "poaching." Sales representatives were allowed to take opportunities from one another, work outside assigned territories, and compete internally instead of collaborating.

On paper, it looked like hustle. In reality, it was a cancer.

It created resentment. Distrust. Territorial behavior. Silence. People stopped sharing. They started protecting.

The first corrective step was not strategy. It was not hiring. It was not technology.

It was **BROT**.

We made a clear, surgical decision:

1. Eliminate poaching entirely
   No working outside territories. No stealing opportunities. Clear ownership.
2. Reward collaboration
   Shared leads were rewarded. Helping teammates was incentivized. Collective success became more important than individual wins.

The change was immediate—and powerful. Trust did not just improve. It accelerated.

Communication increased. Opportunities were shared. The pipeline grew. Deals increased. Energy shifted. People stopped lurking in the dark. They started working together.

This transformation was not just cultural. It was also financial. Sales increased at a staggering rate. The funnel expanded. Execution improved. And eventually, the company was acquired by a Fortune 500 organization at a multiple far beyond expectations. But the most meaningful outcome was not the exit. It was the relationships. Years later, members of that team flew across the country to attend my wedding. Because trust does not end when the job ends. It stays.

The BROT Principle

When you build relationships of trust, performance follows. Always.

Because trust creates:

- safety to speak;
- willingness to collaborate;
- alignment in action;
- energy in execution; and
- Unity.

Unity and BROT in the C.U.R.E.S. Framework

BROT fuels every part of the system:

- **Clarity** → People believe leadership.
- **Unity** → Teams align.
- **Readiness** → People embrace change.
- **Execution** → People give more than minimum effort.
- **Sustainability** → Improvements last.

Trust is not separate from performance. It is what enables it.

Unity is not accidental. It is built intentionally through disciplined leadership actions. It begins with leadership alignment. If leadership is not aligned, nothing else will be.

Incentives must reinforce collaboration. People will always move toward what they are rewarded for.

Communication must be consistent. Alignment is built through repetition, not one-time messaging. Internal competition must be removed. Organizations should compete externally, not internally.

And most importantly, BROT must be built daily. Trust is not built in moments. It is built in habits. Unity is not about getting everyone to agree. It is about getting everyone to move together.

Like a rowing team, where every person pulls in the same direction at the same time, alignment creates acceleration. Without it, effort is wasted. With it, momentum becomes unstoppable.

"Coming together is a beginning, staying together is progress, and working together is success."
— Henry Ford

Everyone benefits from sunlight. Without it, growth dies.

Everyone benefits from trust. Without it, relationships and organizations cannot grow.

That is why: Everyone needs to BROT.

Unity is not agreement; it's alignment in action, built on trust.

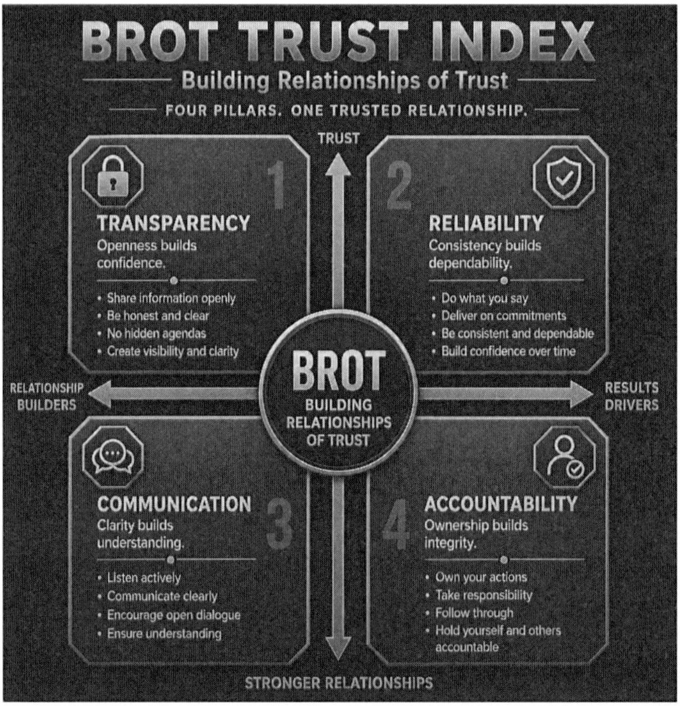

THE FIVE DIMENSIONS OF UNITY

1. Trust (Foundation)
Do people feel safe, respected, and valued?

- Psychological safety

- No fear-based leadership
- Openness and vulnerability

Without trust, Unity is impossible.

2. Alignment (Direction)
Are we rowing in the same direction?

- Shared goals
- Clear priorities
- Organizational clarity tied to Unity

Alignment prevents internal friction.

3. Communication (Connection)
Are we saying the same things the same way?

- Consistent messaging
- Transparency
- Cross-functional clarity

Miscommunication = misalignment.

4. Collaboration (Behavior)
Do teams work together—or compete internally?

- Cross-team cooperation
- Shared wins
- Breaking silos

Unity shows up in how people work together.

5. Accountability (Reinforcement)
Do we hold each other to the standard?

- Peer accountability (not just top-down)
- Ownership of outcomes
- Follow-through

Unity without accountability turns into politeness.

Unity isn't created by structure. It's created by trust, alignment, and accountability in action.

VERY IMPORTANT POINTS

1. Unity is not agreement; it is alignment. It is the difference between people nodding in meetings and people actually moving in the same direction during execution.
2. Misalignment creates energy loss across the organization. When teams are not unified, effort cancels out effort, work gets redone, decisions slow down, and momentum disappears.
3. Trust is the foundation of Unity. Without trust, communication breaks down, alignment disappears, execution slows, and people protect themselves instead of collaborating.
4. BROT—Build Relationships of Trust—is a performance system, not a soft skill. Trust must be built intentionally through leadership alignment, collaboration, consistent communication, and daily habits that reinforce shared success.

CHAPTER 6

READINESS

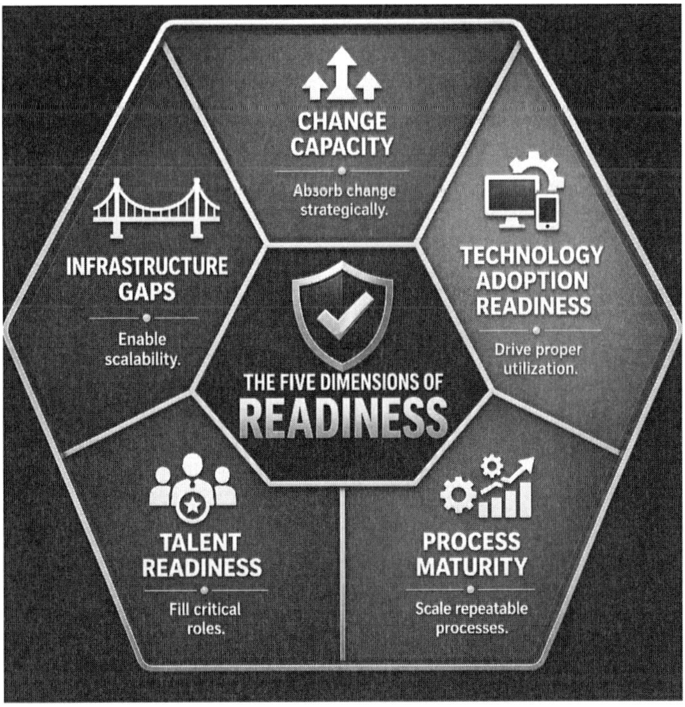

Moving Together, But Can You Sustain It?

We've established something critical: Unity aligns people. Unity creates momentum. Unity gets everyone moving in the same direction. And when Unity is strong, something powerful happens: Organizations accelerate. But acceleration introduces a new question—one that many leaders fail to ask: **"Can your organization handle the speed it's now capable of?"**

Unity creates alignment. But alignment without readiness creates strain.

Teams begin to move faster, but systems lag behind. Decisions improve, but processes begin to break. Momentum builds, but infrastructure starts to crack under pressure.

Unity gets everyone rowing in the same direction. Readiness determines whether the boat can handle the speed.

This is where many organizations make a costly mistake. They celebrate alignment. And immediately push for growth.

But they skip the most important question: Are we actually ready for what we're about to create?

Growth is exciting. New markets. New hires. New technology. New opportunities. And in that excitement, leaders often assume that opportunity equals readiness. It doesn't.

Opportunity exposes your readiness. It doesn't create it.

Organizations don't fail because they lack opportunity. They fail because they try to scale before they are ready to support it.

As John C. Maxwell teaches, "A leader is one who knows the way, goes the way, and shows the way."

But even the best leaders must recognize: Just because the path is clear doesn't mean the organization is prepared to walk it.

Imagine building a 50-story skyscraper. But you only poured a foundation strong enough for 10 stories. At first, everything looks fine. Floors go up. Progress feels fast. Momentum builds. Then something changes. Cracks begin to appear. Stress increases. Instability grows. And eventually, the structure can no longer support itself.

Growth doesn't break organizations. Unprepared growth does.

Most organizations don't collapse because they grow too fast. They collapse because their foundation can't support the growth.

Low readiness does not show up immediately. It shows up under pressure.

You begin to see patterns like:

- constant firefighting;
- burnout across teams;
- technology frustration;
- inconsistent execution;
- hiring faster than onboarding; and
- processes breaking under pressure.

The organization appears to be growing. But underneath, it is struggling to keep up.

Research across high-growth organizations reinforces this reality. Companies that scale without strong process maturity often experience **20 to 30 percent efficiency loss** during growth phases.

Organizations that invest in readiness—across people, processes, and systems—are significantly more likely to sustain long-term growth.

And one of the leading causes of initiative failure? Change saturation. Too much, too fast, without the capacity to absorb it.

Readiness is not one thing. It is built across five critical dimensions. To truly understand readiness, you have to see it as a system, not a checklist.

If even one of these areas is weak, growth doesn't just slow; it creates strain across the entire organization.

The Five Dimensions of Readiness

Readiness is not one thing. It is built across five critical dimensions.

1. Change Capacity
Can your organization absorb change?

When too many initiatives are introduced at once, priorities constantly shift, teams experience change fatigue, and the organization begins to resist—not because it doesn't care, but because it cannot keep up.

Just because leadership can create change doesn't mean the organization can absorb it.

2. Technology Adoption Readiness
Do people actually use the tools you invest in?

Organizations often assume that purchasing technology equals progress. But underutilized systems, poor training, and constant work-arounds tell a different story.

The reality is simple: Technology doesn't fail. Adoption fails.

3. Process Maturity

Are workflows scalable and repeatable?

If processes are not documented, consistent, and efficient under pressure, they will break as the organization grows.

If your process only works when things are calm, it's not a process. It's a hope.

4. Talent Readiness

Do you have the right people in the right roles?

Growth exposes gaps in capability and leadership. Organizations often rely too heavily on a few key individuals, creating risk and limiting scalability.

As Marshall Goldsmith said, "What got you here won't get you there."

5. Infrastructure Gaps

Can your systems support growth?

Reporting, communication, and decision-making structures must scale with the organization. Without them, complexity increases and performance declines.

Growth magnifies weaknesses. It doesn't fix them.

A high-growth e-commerce company I once worked with made an aggressive push to scale. They doubled marketing spend, expanded product lines, and increased order volume rapidly. But they failed to scale the foundation. Fulfillment processes remained unchanged. Customer service capacity lagged. Inventory systems were not upgraded.

The result was predictable. Delays increased. Complaints rose. Refunds grew. Brand reputation suffered.

Revenue increased. But the business weakened.

They didn't outgrow their market. They outgrew their readiness.

Here's another example: A home-health organization rapidly increased its census. But readiness was not in place. Staff was not fully trained. Workflows were not standardized. Technology adoption lagged behind.

The result:

- Compliance risk increased.
- Burnout intensified.
- Quality declined.

Growth did not create the problem. It exposed it.

Low readiness creates compounding costs across the organization.

It leads to:

- burnout;
- inefficiency;
- rework;
- turnover; and
- missed growth opportunities.

These are not isolated issues. They are signals of a system under strain.

Readiness in the C.U.R.E.S. Framework

Clarity gives direction.
Unity creates alignment.
Readiness determines whether the organization can sustain movement.

Alignment without readiness leads to frustration.

How to Build Readiness

Readiness must be built intentionally. It does not happen automatically as organizations grow. It begins with assessment. Before scaling, leaders must evaluate whether the organization is truly prepared. Change must be sequenced. Not everything can happen at once. Priorities must be staged to allow absorption. Foundations must be strengthened before acceleration. Processes, systems, and people must be ready to support growth. Investment must focus on adoption, not just acquisition, especially when it comes to technology. And capacity must be built intentionally, ensuring that the organization can handle what is coming next.

The Hidden Truth About Readiness

Readiness requires discipline. It requires leaders to say something that many organizations struggle to say: "Not yet." Because the hardest truth is this: Just because you can scale doesn't mean you should.

This brings us to the next phase: Even with clarity, unity, and readiness in place, execution still determines results.

Being ready doesn't guarantee success, but not being ready guarantees struggle.

A skyscraper does not fail because it is tall. It fails because its foundation is not strong enough. Organizations are no different.

If you want to grow higher, you must first build deeper.

Just because you can grow doesn't mean you're ready to.

Being ready doesn't guarantee success, but not being ready guarantees struggle.

VERY IMPORTANT POINTS

1. Unity creates momentum, but Readiness determines whether the organization can handle it. Alignment gets people moving together; but without the right foundation, faster movement creates strain instead of sustainable growth.
2. Opportunity exposes readiness; it does not create it. Organizations often assume growth means they are ready; but scaling before people, processes, and systems are prepared can weaken the business.
3. Low readiness shows up under pressure. Firefighting, burnout, technology frustration, inconsistent execution, weak onboarding, and broken processes are all signs that the organization's foundation cannot support the speed of growth.
4. Readiness must be built intentionally across five dimensions. Sustainable growth requires change capacity, technology adoption readiness, process maturity, talent readiness, and infrastructure that can scale with the organization.

CHAPTER 7

EXECUTION

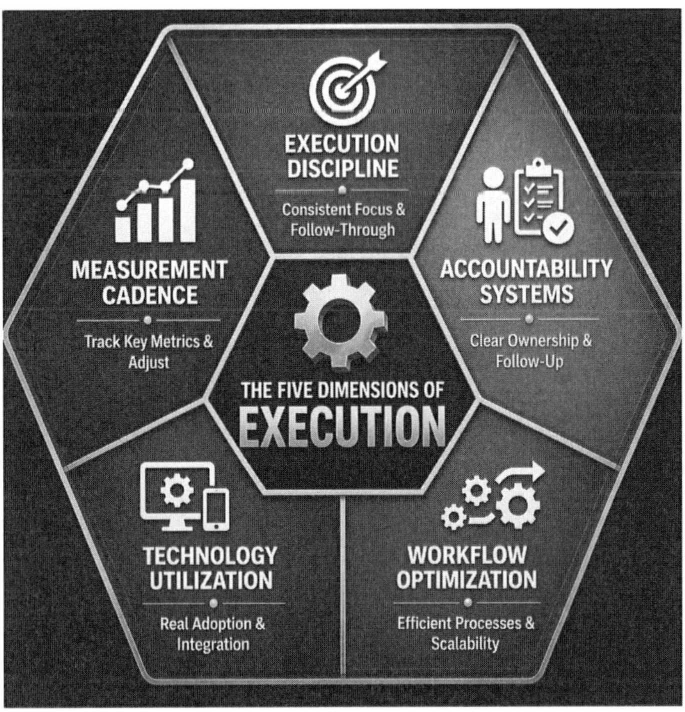

Built for It; But Are You Doing It?

In Chapter 6, we asked a critical question: "Is your organization ready to scale?"

- Do you have the people?
- The processes?
- The infrastructure?
- The capacity to absorb change?

Let's assume the answer is yes.

You have Clarity.
You have Unity.
You have Readiness.

Everything is aligned.
Everything is in place.

So why do so many organizations still struggle? There is a gap that exists between preparation and performance. A gap between knowing and winning.

Being ready doesn't create results. Execution does.

Readiness prepares you. Execution delivers.

Picture this: You're driving on I-15 near Fillmore, Utah. The road is long and straight. Visibility is clear. The speed limit is 80 miles per hour. Everything about the environment is built for speed.

Now imagine two organizations operating on that exact same road.

Organization A has strong systems, clear workflows, high accountability, and fully utilized technology. They are moving at 80 miles per hour.

Organization B operates in the same market, with the same opportunity, on the same road. But they are driving with a donut spare tire.

What happens?

Their maximum speed is cut in half. They hesitate. They avoid pushing too hard. And slowly, they begin falling behind, despite having access to the same opportunity.

Nothing about the environment changed. Only their ability to execute did.

You can be on an 80-mph road and still be a 40-mph company.

Execution is one of the most misunderstood concepts in business. It is often confused with activity. With effort. With motion. But execution is not about being busy. Execution is about doing what matters most—consistently, at a high level, over time.

As Thomas Edison said, "Vision without execution is hallucination."

Execution is where strategy becomes reality.

Execution problems rarely show up as laziness. They show up as inconsistency.

You begin to see patterns like:

- constant busyness with little progress;
- projects that never fully complete;
- leaders revisiting the same issues repeatedly;
- technology that exists but isn't used; and
- accountability that is inconsistent.

The organization appears active. But it is not effective.

Across industries, the data tells a consistent story.

Only about 60 percent of strategic initiatives are successfully executed in most organizations. Poor execution can reduce productivity by 20 to 40 percent. And companies with strong execution discipline consistently outperform their peers in both profitability and growth.

Execution is not a minor issue. It is the difference between potential and performance.

Execution is not accidental. It is built across five core pillars that determine whether an organization can consistently deliver results.

If you want to understand why execution breaks down, you have to see it as a system, not a behavior.

When even one of these pillars is weak, execution doesn't just slow; it becomes inconsistent.

The Five Pillars of Execution

1. Execution Discipline

Execution begins with discipline. It is the ability to consistently do what you said you would do—especially when it is inconvenient. It requires focus, follow-through, and consistency.

Execution is the discipline of doing the right things—even when it's not convenient.

2. Accountability Systems

Execution cannot exist without accountability. Ownership must be clear. Follow-up must be consistent. And outcomes—both positive and negative—must be reinforced.

As Stephen Covey said, "Accountability breeds response-ability."

Without accountability, execution becomes optional.

3. Workflow Optimization

Execution depends on how work flows through the organization. If processes are inefficient, inconsistent, or unclear, execution slows down—no matter how talented the team is.

If your workflow slows you down, your growth will expose it.

4. Technology Utilization

Most organizations believe they have a technology problem. They don't. They have a technology utilization problem. Execution requires that tools are not just purchased, but actually used, integrated, and embedded into daily workflows. Adoption matters more than acquisition.

5. Measurement Cadence
What gets measured gets managed. And what gets managed gets improved.

Or, as Peter Drucker said, "What gets measured gets improved."

Execution requires consistent tracking of what matters—through KPIs, regular reviews, and data-driven decisions.

I once observed a mid-sized company that had everything it needed to succeed. Strong strategy. Talented leadership. Clear market opportunity. But execution was inconsistent. Weekly priorities were unclear. Accountability was not enforced. KPIs were not reviewed regularly.

The result was predictable. Projects stalled. Teams worked hard, but inconsistently. Revenue plateaued.

The diagnosis was not a strategy problem. It was not a talent problem. It was an execution problem.

Here's another example: A hospice organization implemented significant improvements:

- A new EMR
- Updated workflows
- Enhanced compliance processes

But execution broke down. Staff did not consistently follow processes. Leadership did not enforce accountability. Metrics were not reviewed regularly.

The result:

- Documentation inconsistency
- Increased compliance risk
- Lost efficiency

The system existed. But execution didn't.

Poor execution creates compounding organizational damage.

It leads to:

- lost revenue;
- wasted effort;
- frustration;
- burnout; and
- missed opportunities.

Execution gaps are expensive. And often invisible, until the impact becomes too large to ignore.

Execution in the C.U.R.E.S. Framework

Clarity shows the path.
Unity aligns people.
Readiness prepares the system.
Execution is where results are created.

Ideas don't create outcomes. Execution does.

How to Improve Execution

Execution improves through discipline, not inspiration. It starts by narrowing the focus. Fewer priorities create stronger execution. Ownership must be clear, one owner per outcome. Accountability must be built into regular rhythms, including weekly check-ins and progress reviews. Workflows must be optimized by removing friction and standardizing processes. And measurement must be relentless, tracking what matters and adjusting quickly when performance drifts.

Execution is not complicated. But it is difficult. Because it requires consistency.

Execution is not glamorous. It is repetitive. It is disciplined. It is consistent. And that is exactly why so many organizations struggle with it.

Most organizations don't fail because they don't know what to do. They fail because they don't consistently do it.

Execution creates results. But it raises the final question: "Can you sustain them?"

Ideas don't create outcomes. Execution does.

Because execution can win the game. But sustainability determines how long you stay winning. You can have the best strategy, the best people, and the best systems. But if you are operating like a 40-mph organization on an 80-mph road, you will never reach your full potential.

Winning is not about knowing what to do. It is about doing it, consistently, completely, and at speed.

Execution turns potential into performance and performance into results.

VERY IMPORTANT POINTS

1. Being ready doesn't create results; execution does. Readiness prepares the organization, but execution is what turns strategy, alignment, and capability into measurable performance.
2. Execution is not activity; it is disciplined consistency. Busy teams are not always effective teams. True execution means doing what matters most, consistently and at a high level over time.
3. Execution breaks down when systems are inconsistent. Unclear priorities, weak accountability, underused technology, inefficient workflows, and irregular measurement all create execution gaps that slow performance.
4. Strong execution is built on five pillars. Execution discipline, accountability systems, workflow optimization, technology utilization, and measurement cadence determine whether an organization can consistently deliver results.

CHAPTER 8

SUSTAINABILITY

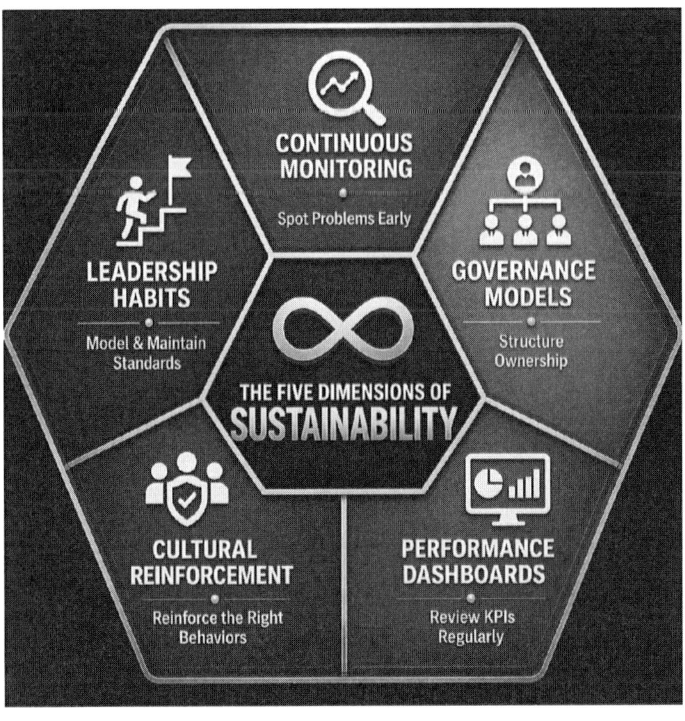

Why Winning Once Isn't Enough

Execution creates results. That's where most organizations celebrate. A big quarter. A successful initiative. A breakthrough moment. Growth. Momentum. Energy.

And in that moment, it feels like you've arrived.

But here's the reality most organizations don't fully understand:

Execution can win the game.
Sustainability determines how long you stay winning.

Because the real test of an organization is not whether it can succeed once. It's whether it can do it again. And again. And again.

Think about the music industry.

There are artists who produce one hit song, something that dominates the charts, captures attention, and creates a moment. And then they disappear.

Artists like Vanilla Ice with "Ice Ice Baby," or Sir Mix-a-Lot with "Baby Got Back" created massive cultural moments. But those moments didn't last.

Now compare that to bands like The Beatles or Queen. They didn't just create hits. They created systems. They built processes, collaboration, discipline, and creative consistency that allowed them to produce excellence over time.

If you want your organization to be remembered like the Beatles, you don't chase hits. You build systems that create them, again and again.

That is sustainability.

Most organizations operate like one-hit wonders.

They achieve success through:

- a strong push;
- a talented leader;
- a focused initiative; or
- a moment of alignment.

And for a time, it works. But without systems to support that success, it fades. Momentum slows. Old habits return. Performance declines. And leadership asks, "What happened?"

Sustainability is not about maintaining effort. It's about maintaining systems. Because effort fades. Energy fluctuates. People change.

But systems—systems create consistency.

If sustainability is driven by systems, then the next question becomes, "What are those systems?" Because sustainable organizations don't rely on effort, motivation, or moments; they rely on structure. And that structure shows up in five critical areas.

As W. Edwards Deming taught, "A bad system will beat a good person every time."

The inverse is also true: A strong system will sustain strong performance—even as individuals change.

The Symptoms of Low Sustainability

Organizations that lack sustainability don't fail immediately. They regress.

You begin to see patterns like:

- initiatives that succeed once but never repeat;
- teams that revert to old behaviors;
- improvements that fade over time;
- constant need to "restart" progress; and
- leadership frustration around inconsistency.

The organization is not broken. It is unstable. This is one of the most expensive problems in business, and one of the least visible. Because success still happens. Just not consistently.

The costs show up as:

- rework;

- retraining;
- reinvestment; and
- rebuilding.

You're not investing once. You're paying for the same improvement—over and over again.

You're not losing because you can't succeed. You're losing because you can't sustain success.

Sustainability in the C.U.R.E.S. Framework

Clarity defines direction.
Unity aligns people.
Readiness prepares the system.
Execution delivers results.
Sustainability ensures those results last.

Without sustainability:

- **Clarity** fades
- **Unity** weakens
- **Readiness** resets
- **Execution** becomes inconsistent

Everything you built slips.

This is what most organizations miss. Sustainability is not one thing. It's a system. And like any system, it is only as strong as its weakest part. You can have strong execution, but without measurement, it fades. You can have strong culture, but without leadership reinforcement, it drifts. You can have great dashboards, but without governance, nothing changes.

Sustainability doesn't break all at once. It breaks at the weakest point in the system.

The Five Drivers of a Sustainability System

Sustainability is not accidental. It is built intentionally across five key drivers:

1. Continuous Monitoring
Sustainable organizations don't assume things are working. They verify it. They track performance consistently, identify early warning signs, and adjust before problems grow.

2. Governance Models
There must be structure behind success. Clear ownership. Defined accountability. Decision-making frameworks. Without governance, success becomes dependent on individuals instead of systems.

3. Performance Dashboards
Visibility drives consistency. Organizations that sustain results know what matters—and they measure it regularly. Not occasionally. Not reactively. Consistently.

4. Cultural Reinforcement
Culture is what happens repeatedly. Not what is said once. Sustainable organizations reinforce behaviors through recognition, accountability, and leadership modeling. They don't just define culture. They live it.

As Peter Drucker famously said, "Culture eats strategy for breakfast."

And sustainability depends on culture.

5. Leadership Habits
Leadership is the multiplier.

Sustainable organizations have leaders who consistently:

- reinforce priorities;
- model behaviors;
- maintain discipline; and
- stay aligned.

Because systems don't sustain themselves. Leaders sustain them.

I've seen organizations achieve incredible results. Revenue growth. Operational improvement. Cultural transformation. And then, within six to twelve months, they are back where they started. Not because the strategy was wrong. Not because the people changed. But because the systems to sustain the improvement were never built.

Sustainability is less exciting than execution. It's not flashy. It doesn't create immediate headlines.

It's repetitive.

It's disciplined.

It's consistent.

And that's exactly why most organizations struggle with it.

Most organizations don't fail because they can't improve. They fail because they can't maintain improvement.

The C.U.R.E.S. Conclusion

This is where everything comes together.

Clarity without Unity creates confusion.

Unity without Readiness creates strain.

Readiness without Execution creates delay.

Execution without Sustainability creates temporary success.

But when all five work together, you don't just improve. You transform.

And more importantly, you sustain it.

Anyone can have a good quarter. Anyone can launch a successful initiative. Anyone can create a moment of success. But very few organizations can create sustained excellence. Because that requires something different. It requires systems.

Winning once proves you can do it. Sustaining it proves who you are.

VERY IMPORTANT POINTS

1. Execution can win the game, but Sustainability determines how long you stay winning. The real test is not whether an organization can succeed once, but whether it can repeat success again and again.
2. Sustainability depends on systems, not short bursts of effort. Effort fades, energy fluctuates, and people change, but strong systems create consistency over time.
3. Low sustainability causes organizations to regress. When improvements fade, old habits return, initiatives have to be restarted, and leaders repeatedly pay for the same progress, the issue is not lack of success—it is lack of sustained success.
4. Sustainability is built through five key drivers. Continuous monitoring, governance models, performance dashboards, cultural reinforcement, and leadership habits keep results from fading and turn improvement into lasting transformation.

ONE SYSTEM.
FIVE PILLARS.
UNLIMITED POTENTIAL.
Stronger Teams Built on Unity
Clear Direction Aligned to Purpose
Consistent Execution Driving Results
Sustainable Growth That Lasts
SUSTAINABILITY
SUSTAIN IT. STRENGTHEN IT. SCALE IT.
Continuous Monitoring
Spot Problems Early
Governance Models
Structure Ownership
Performance Dashboards
Review KPIs Regularly
Cultural Reinforcement
Reinforce the Right Behaviors
Leadership Habits
Model & Maintain Standards
CLARITY
SEE IT. ALIGN IT. LIVE IT.
Strategic Clarity
Clear direction & Measurable Outcomes
Role Clarity
Defined Ownership & Responsibilities
Operational Clarity
Standard Workflows & Consistency
Communication Clarity
Clear Expectations & No Mixed Signals
Technology Clarity
Proper Utilization & Defined Use Cases
UNITY
TOGETHER. UNITED. UNSTOPPABLE.
Trust
Openness & Vulnerability
Alignment
Shared Goals & Clear Priorities
Communication
Consistent Messaging & Transparency
Collaboration
Cross-Team Cooperation & Breaking Silos
Accountability
Ownership of Outcomes & Follow-through
THE C.U.R.E.S. FRAMEWORK
A Unified System for Organizational Health, Performance & Sustainable Growth
EXECUTION
FOCUS. EXECUTE. ACHIEVE.
Execution Discipline
Consistent Focus & Follow-Through
Accountability Systems
Clear Ownership & Follow-Up
Measurement Cadence
Track Key Metrics & Adjust
Technology Utilization
Real Adoption & Integration
Workflow Optimization
Efficient Processes & Scalability
READINESS
PREPARE. EQUIP. EMPOWER.
People Readiness
Right People, Right Roles & Right Mindset
Leadership Readiness
Capable Leaders at Every Level
Process Readiness
Documented, Efficient & Scalable Processes
Resource Readiness
Right Tools, Time & Budget in Place
Culture Readiness
Aligned Culture that Drives Change
C.U.R.E.S.
THE FOUNDATION OF ORGANIZATIONAL EXCELLENCE
C CLARITY See it. Align it. Live it.
U UNITY Together. United. Unstoppable.
R READINESS Prepare. Equip. Empower.
E EXECUTION Focus. Execute. Achieve.
S SUSTAINABILITY Sustain it. Strengthen it. Scale it.
CLARITY CREATES DIRECTION. UNITY CREATES STRENGTH. READINESS CREATES CAPACITY.
EXECUTION CREATES. RESULTS. SUSTAINABILITY CREATES LEGACY.
TOGETHER, C.U.R.E.S. CREATES AN ORGANIZATION THAT THRIVES.

CHAPTER 9

THE POST-TREATMENT ORGANIZATION

What Healthy Organizations Actually Look Like

Now we move to something even more important:

What does a truly healthy organization actually look like?

Because once you've:

- diagnosed the cancers;
- treated the root causes; and
- built systems for sustainability,

you don't just survive. You transform.

The goal of *The Corporate Cure* isn't just to remove dysfunction. It's to build an organization that thrives without it.

When I think about my mom and her real medical treatment, I'm reminded of something important. At first, the focus is survival. Remove the threat. Stabilize the system. Protect what matters most. But recovery doesn't stop there. Recovery is not just about removing what was wrong. It's about rebuilding strength.

Energy returns. Confidence grows. Systems begin functioning the way they were meant to. Life expands again. The same is true in organizations. A post-treatment organization doesn't just eliminate problems. It operates at an entirely different level. It is no longer defined by what it was trying to fix. It is defined by how it now performs. One of the most striking differences is not just what you see. It's what you feel. You can walk into a healthy organization and sense it almost immediately.

In unhealthy organizations:

- meetings feel tense;
- decisions feel unclear;
- teams operate in silos; and
- energy is reactive.

In healthy organizations:

- conversations are open;
- decisions are clear;
- teams move together; and
- energy is proactive.

Healthy organizations don't feel chaotic. They feel aligned.

As leadership expert Patrick Lencioni emphasizes, "Not finance. Not strategy. Not technology. It is teamwork that remains the ultimate competitive advantage." And teamwork is the result of organizational health.

What Healthy Organizations Actually *Look* Like

Health is not abstract. It is visible. It shows up in consistent, repeatable patterns across the organization.

1. Clarity Is Obvious
In healthy organizations, clarity is not something people debate. It is something they experience.

Everyone understands:

- where the organization is going;
- what matters most; and
- what success looks like.

There is no confusion. No competing priorities. No guessing.

When clarity exists, speed follows.

2. Unity Is Real (Not Forced)
Alignment is not manufactured. It is natural. Teams collaborate without friction. Information flows freely. People support each other because they trust each other. There is no internal competition. No hidden agendas.

Alignment isn't announced; it's demonstrated.

3. Readiness Is Built In
Healthy organizations are not caught off guard by growth. They are built for it. Systems support scale. People can handle increased demand.

Change does not break the organization. It adapts. The organization doesn't just grow. It is designed to grow.

4. Execution Is Consistent
Execution is no longer sporadic. It is dependable. Priorities are followed through. Accountability is clear. Work gets done. Not occasionally. Consistently.

5. Sustainability Is Natural
Success is no longer fragile. It is repeatable. Systems reinforce behavior. Performance does not rely on heroics. Results are not one-time events. They are patterns.

Great organizations don't rely on effort. They rely on systems.

As Indra Nooyi, former CEO of PepsiCo, said, "Performance with purpose is how you deliver sustained success."

Sustainability is not accidental. It is built.

Leading Indicators of Recovery

Healthy organizations don't just show results. They show signals, before the results even appear. These are the early indicators that transformation is taking hold:

1. People Start Speaking Up
You begin to hear more ideas. More feedback. More healthy debate. Truth returns to the organization.

2. Collaboration Increases
Teams begin working together. Silos break down. Shared wins become visible.

3. Decisions Improve
They become faster. More informed. More aligned.

4. Energy Shifts
Stress decreases. Ownership increases. Engagement rises.

Recovery shows up in behavior before it shows up in numbers.

The Scalable Operating Model

Where Everything Comes Together

This is where transformation becomes undeniable. A post-treatment organization doesn't just function well. It scales well.

What that looks like:

Growth no longer breaks the system. More clients do not create chaos. Processes hold under pressure. New team members ramp faster because expectations are clear, onboarding is structured, and workflows are defined. Leaders shift from firefighting to leading. They spend less time reacting and more time thinking strategically. Performance becomes predictable. Results are consistent. Outcomes are measurable.

If growth creates chaos, your system isn't ready.

We worked with a company that had everything going for it:

- Strong demand
- A great product
- A growing market

But internally, the organization was struggling. Systems were inconsistent. Teams were not aligned. Execution varied across departments.

After applying the C.U.R.E.S. framework:

- clarity improved;
- incentives aligned;
- processes were streamlined; and
- accountability increased.

The result?

Faster growth. Higher margins. A better employee experience.

They didn't just grow. They became capable of growth.

Healthy organizations are not perfect.

They still experience:

- challenges;
- change; and
- pressure.

But they respond differently. They detect problems early. They address root causes. They adapt quickly. They stay aligned.

The goal is not to build an organization that never struggles, but one that always recovers. You can feel the difference between a healthy and an unhealthy organization, but you can also see it. Because organizational health isn't abstract. It shows up in clear, observable patterns.

Now that we understand what a healthy organization looks like, the next question becomes: **How do you build this—intentionally, consistently, and at scale?**

Because transformation is not a one-time event. It is a repeatable process.

A healthy organization is not defined by the absence of problems. It is defined by how it responds to them.

Healthy organizations don't avoid challenges. They outgrow them.

VERY IMPORTANT POINTS

1. A healthy organization is defined by how it performs after dysfunction is removed. The goal of *The Corporate Cure* is not just to eliminate problems, but to build an organization that operates at a stronger, more aligned, and more sustainable level.
2. Healthy organizations feel different because they operate differently. Conversations are open, decisions are clear, teams move together, and energy becomes proactive instead of reactive.
3. Organizational health shows up in repeatable patterns. Clarity is obvious, Unity is real, Readiness is built in, Execution is consistent, and Sustainability becomes natural.
4. Healthy organizations do not avoid problems; they recover faster. They detect issues early, address root causes, adapt quickly, and stay aligned under pressure.

CHAPTER 10

BUILDING AN EARLY DETECTION SYSTEM

How Great Organizations Stay Healthy

In Chapter 9, we answered an important question: What does a healthy organization look like? Now we answer the most important question of all: **How do you keep it that way?**

Because here is the truth most leaders eventually learn: You don't build a great organization once. You maintain it continuously.

The best organizations don't avoid problems. They detect them early and address them quickly.

Health is not an outcome. It is a discipline.

There is a simple question often asked when facing something overwhelming: How do you eat an elephant?

The answer is simple: One bite at a time.

The same is true for building a great organization.

When leaders look at everything that needs to be improved—culture, systems, technology, alignment, performance—it can feel overwhelming.

Too many moving parts. Too many problems. Too much to fix. And when everything feels big, nothing changes. But the shift is this: You don't fix everything at once.

You build a system that allows you to:

- see clearly;
- act consistently; and
- improve continuously.

Great organizations aren't built in one transformation. They're built through consistent, intentional progress.

As James Clear writes, "You do not rise to the level of your goals. You fall to the level of your systems."

That is what this chapter is about. This is what separates great organizations from average ones.

Not strategy.

Not talent.

Not even execution.

But the ability to detect, diagnose, and correct, early.

An Early Detection System is what turns leadership from reactive into proactive.

It is what separates organizations that respond to problems from organizations that prevent them. An Early Detection System allows you to:

- identify issues before they become problems;
- detect organizational cancers early;
- maintain alignment across teams; and
- sustain performance over time.

It changes everything. Because now, instead of reacting to breakdowns, you are preventing them.

The Five Components of an Early Detection System

Like everything in this book, this is not one thing. It is a system.

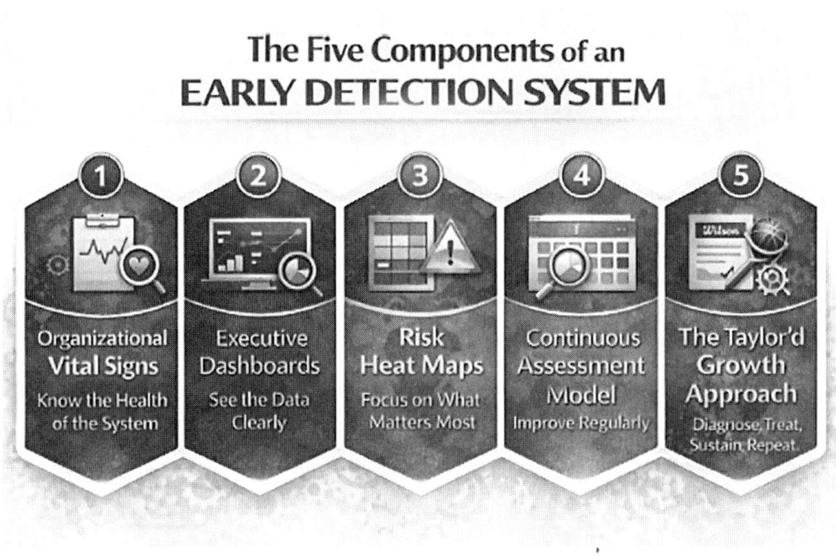

1. Organizational Vital Signs

Know the Health of the System
Every healthy system monitors key indicators. The human body tracks heart rate, blood pressure, oxygen levels—because without visibility, there is no control. Your organization must do the same.

You must track your core vital signs:

- **Clarity** → Do people know where we're going?
- **Unity (BROT)** → Are we working together? Do people trust each other?
- **Readiness** → Can we handle what's coming?
- **Execution** → Are we delivering results?
- **Sustainability** → Can we maintain performance?

What gets measured gets managed. What gets ignored becomes a problem.

As Peter Drucker taught, "You can't manage what you don't measure."

2. Executive Dashboards

From Guessing to Seeing
Healthy organizations don't guess. They see.

An Executive Dashboard brings everything together:

- C.U.R.E.S. scores
- BROT Trust Index
- Organizational Health Index (OHI)

- Trend lines over time

This creates something powerful: visibility.

With visibility comes:

- faster decision-making;
- clear prioritization; and
- alignment across leadership.

Leaders shouldn't rely on instincts alone. They should rely on insight.

3. Risk Heat Maps

Focus on What Matters Most

Not all problems are equal. Some are small and contained. Others are systemic and spreading.

Risk Heat Maps help you see:

- where organizational cancers exist;
- how severe they are; and
- where to act first.

Because great organizations don't try to fix everything. They focus on what matters most, first.

You don't treat everything. You treat what matters most.

4. Continuous Assessment Model

Health Is Not a One-Time Check

Most organizations assess once. Great organizations assess continuously.

They build rhythms of evaluation:

- Quarterly diagnostics
- Leadership reviews
- Team-level assessments
- Ongoing feedback loops

This creates:

- early detection;
- faster correction; and
- continuous improvement.

The goal isn't perfection; it's progress.

As Carol Dweck teaches, "Becoming is better than being."

Growth is not an event. It is a process.

5. The Taylor'd Growth Approach

Diagnose. Treat. Sustain. Repeat.
The Taylor'd Growth approach is built on one core belief:

Organizations don't fail because they lack effort. They fail because they lack alignment and visibility.

The model is simple. And powerful.

Step 1: Diagnose
Identify organizational cancers.
Use scorecards and dashboards to see clearly.

Step 2: Prioritize
Use risk heat maps.
Focus on the highest-impact areas.

Step 3: Treat
Apply C.U.R.E.S.
Fix root causes, not symptoms.

Step 4: Sustain
Build systems.
Reinforce behaviors.
Monitor continuously.

Why This Works

Because it transforms the way organizations operate.

It turns:

- complexity → clarity;
- reaction → proaction; and
- effort → results.

And it gives leaders something they rarely have: **control with visibility.**

The Final Shift

Most organizations believe, "We just need to work harder."

But the truth is: You don't need more effort. You need a better system.

If you take one thing from this book, let it be this:

Great organizations are not built by accident. They are built by design.

You don't need:

- a perfect team;
- a perfect strategy; or
- a perfect moment.

You need:

- the willingness to see clearly;
- the courage to address truth; and
- the discipline to build systems.

The First Step

You don't fix everything today. You don't transform overnight.

You take one step.

You identify one gap.

You fix one system.

You improve one area.

And then you repeat.

The journey to a great organization doesn't happen all at once. It happens one decision, one action, one improvement at a time.

You don't need to rebuild your organization overnight. You just need to start. Because the organizations that win are not the ones that wait. They are the ones that act.

You don't need more time.
You don't need better circumstances.
You don't need a perfect plan.

You need to begin.

See clearly.
Align your people.
Prepare your system.
Execute with discipline.
Sustain what works.

And then…

Do it again.

— The C.U.R.E.S. Framework

The ***CURE*** isn't temporary. It's a new way to operate.

VERY IMPORTANT POINTS

1. Great organizations stay healthy through continuous detection, not one-time transformation. Organizational health is not a single outcome; it is a discipline built through consistent visibility, diagnosis, correction, and improvement.
2. An Early Detection System turns leadership from reactive to proactive. Instead of waiting for breakdowns, leaders can identify issues early, detect organizational cancers, maintain alignment, and sustain performance over time.
3. The system depends on five key components. Organizational Vital Signs, Executive Dashboards, Risk Heat Maps, a Continuous Assessment Model, and the Taylor'd Growth Approach give leaders the visibility and structure needed to act wisely.
4. The CURE is not temporary; it is a new way to operate. Healthy organizations repeatedly diagnose, prioritize, treat, and sustain—turning complexity into clarity, reaction into proaction, and effort into results.

APPENDIX

FEAR-BASED LEADERSHIP

Fear is one of the most misunderstood forces in leadership. At first glance, it can look like accountability. It can feel like urgency. It can even resemble high standards. In the short term, it may appear to produce results. Deadlines are met. Activity increases. People respond quickly. But over time, something very different begins to happen.

Fear behaves exactly like cancer. It spreads quietly. It reshapes behavior. And it slowly destroys the very elements that make organizations great. What once looked like discipline becomes tension. What once looked like performance becomes survival.

As Amy Edmondson, a leading researcher on psychological safety, has shown, "The best teams are not the ones where people never make mistakes, but the ones where people feel safe enough to admit them."

Fear eliminates that safety.

I once worked as the VP of Sales under a CEO who believed deeply in accountability.

Every quarter, we held QBRs (Quarterly Business Reviews), where each sales representative would stand in front of the entire organization and walk through their activity, their results, what worked, and what didn't.

On paper, it was a great practice.

It created:

- visibility;
- learning;
- ownership; and
- continuous improvement.

When done correctly, this is one of the most powerful disciplines an organization can have. It allows teams to learn from one another, identify patterns, and continuously improve performance. But that's not what this became.

This CEO, let's call him Biff, had a very different objective. In his mind, a QBR wasn't successful unless someone broke down. Publicly. Emotionally. He didn't just review performance; he looked for someone to tear down.

He would:

- press relentlessly;
- highlight weaknesses in front of peers; and
- push until the individual cracked.

And when they did, he saw it as success. In his mind, the logic was simple: If people fear being in that position, they'll work harder to avoid it. And for a small number of individuals, that may have been true. But for the organization as a whole, the impact was devastating. People stopped approaching QBRs as an opportunity to learn. They no longer asked, *What can I improve?* Instead, they asked, *How do I survive this?*

That subtle shift changed everything.

Over time, the effects became undeniable:

- People shared less openly.
- Risk-taking disappeared.
- Collaboration dropped.
- Energy declined.

And most importantly, trust eroded.

In another organization, fear showed up in a different, but equally destructive, way.

During a company-wide call, an employee accidentally came off mute and was heard saying: "We have way too many meetings." It wasn't malicious. It wasn't even inaccurate. In fact, it reflected what most people in the organization were already thinking. He was simply the one who said it out loud. By the end of the day, he was fired. The message spread instantly, without needing to be spoken: Don't say the wrong thing.

From that moment forward, behavior changed:

- People stopped speaking up.
- Ideas stopped being shared.

- Feedback disappeared.
- Meetings became quieter, and far less productive.

The same few voices dominated every conversation, while everyone else remained silent.

Fear doesn't destroy performance immediately. It destroys truth first.

And once truth disappears, everything else follows.

- Bad ideas go unchallenged.
- Poor decisions go unchecked.
- Innovation slows.
- Engagement drops.
- Leadership becomes disconnected from reality.

The organization doesn't become high performing. It becomes highly controlled.

Fear-based leadership directly impacts the core of the C.U.R.E.S. framework.

Unity is destroyed because trust cannot exist in an environment of fear. Alignment becomes superficial at best.

Execution weakens because people focus on doing just enough to avoid negative attention rather than striving for excellence.

Sustainability becomes impossible because real issues are never surfaced, addressed, or resolved.

Over time, fear spreads through the organization, shaping behavior at every level.

Severity: High (Fast-Spreading Cultural Cancer)

This is a high-severity cancer because it spreads quickly and embeds deeply into culture. It is reinforced through behavior, amplified through leadership, and learned through experience. And once it takes hold, it is difficult to reverse without intentional intervention.

When fear enters the room, truth leaves it.

Treatment Plan (C.U.R.E.S.)

The solution is not to remove accountability. It is to remove fear from how accountability is delivered. Organizations must create environments where truth can surface without consequence. This requires a shift toward psychological safety, where individuals feel comfortable sharing ideas, raising concerns, and admitting mistakes. Accountability must become constructive rather than punitive. The goal is not to expose weaknesses, but to improve performance.

Leaders must intentionally build trust by reinforcing transparency, rewarding honesty, and modeling vulnerability. When leaders admit mistakes and accept feedback, they create permission for others to do the same. And perhaps most importantly, organizations must begin rewarding truth, not perfection.

If people are afraid to speak, you're not leading—you're controlling.

Fear-based leadership doesn't just limit performance. It limits reality. When people stop speaking the truth, leaders lose access to the information they need to make good decisions. And when that happens, the organization begins operating in a version of reality that no longer reflects what is actually happening.

Like all organizational cancers, fear-based leadership begins subtly. It grows through behavior, spreads through culture, and reshapes how people interact over time. Left untreated, it becomes the norm. And once it becomes the norm, it defines the organization.

Fear may create short-term compliance, but it will always destroy long-term performance. Because organizations do not grow when people are afraid. They grow when people are engaged, safe to contribute, willing to challenge, and invested in the outcome.

Fear may drive compliance, but it kills commitment.

EGO-DRIVEN LEADERSHIP

When the Leader Becomes the Limiting Factor

Ego-driven leadership is one of the most dangerous cancers in an organization, not because it is loud or obvious, but because it is often invisible to the person causing it.

Unlike fear-based leadership, which tends to reveal itself through tension and discomfort, ego-driven leadership hides behind language that sounds healthy. Leaders often position themselves as open, collaborative, and inclusive. They say things like:

- "I have an open-door policy."
- "I welcome feedback."
- "May the best idea win."

On the surface, these statements reflect strong leadership principles. They signal openness, humility, and a desire for collective success. But in reality, they are often not lived out.

As Jim Collins observed in *Good to Great*, "The most effective leaders build enduring greatness through a paradoxical blend of personal humility and professional will."

Ego-driven leadership lacks humility, and without humility, truth struggles to survive.

Unfortunately, I have seen this cancer firsthand at more than one organization, and often at the highest levels of leadership. These were not bad people. In fact, many of them genuinely believed they were strong, open leaders. They said all the right things. They encouraged feedback. They invited ideas. They talked about collaboration and alignment.

They would say:

- "Bring me your ideas."
- "Challenge me."
- "We want the best thinking."

But when the moment came for those ideas to actually be shared, the reality told a very different story. Ideas were only accepted if they aligned with what the leader had already decided. Feedback that challenged direction was quickly dismissed. And in some cases, ideas were not just rejected—they were publicly criticized.

They were labeled as:

- not thought out;
- misguided; or
- even stupid.

And when that happens in a public setting, something powerful takes place. Everyone sees it. Everyone learns.

Organizations are incredibly adaptive. When people observe behavior, they adjust. Not intentionally. Not maliciously. But predictably.

People begin to ask themselves a different question. Rather than asking, *Is this idea good?* they ask, *Does it match what leadership already believes?*

That shift changes everything. Because when people stop evaluating ideas based on merit and instead evaluate them based on alignment with leadership, innovation begins to disappear. Over time, behavior changes in very specific ways:

- People stop sharing real ideas.
- Only "safe" ideas are voiced.
- Constructive tension disappears.

And a new pattern emerges: Ego alignment replaces organizational alignment.

You begin to see:

- performative agreement;
- "butt-kissing" behaviors;
- people saying what leaders want to hear; and
- people not saying what the organization actually needs to hear.

People are no longer speaking truth. They are speaking survival.

Over time, the damage compounds across the organization:

- Poor decisions go unchallenged.
- Good ideas never surface.
- High performers disengage or leave.
- Innovation slows.
- Stagnation takes hold.

The organization may appear aligned on the surface. But underneath, it is anything but.

The organization doesn't become aligned. It becomes compliant.

Ego-driven leadership doesn't just affect culture. It breaks the foundation of performance.

Within the C.U.R.E.S. framework:

- **Clarity** becomes distorted, because decisions are filtered through a single perspective.
- **Unity** becomes artificial, because alignment is based on agreement, not truth.
- **Execution** suffers, because flawed decisions go unchallenged.

From a BROT (Build Relationships of Trust) perspective, the impact is equally significant: Trust erodes quickly.

Because people begin to realize, "It's not safe to disagree here."
And when it's not safe to disagree, it's not possible to improve.

Severity: High (Leadership-Centric Cancer)

This is a high-severity cancer because it originates at the top. And what happens at the top spreads everywhere.

It:

- impacts every department;
- influences every decision; and
- multiplies other organizational cancers.

If the leader can't hear truth, the organization can't improve.

Treatment Plan (C.U.R.E.S.)

Ego-driven leadership cannot be corrected with surface-level adjustments. It requires intentional transformation, both in mindset and in behavior. The first step is building real feedback systems, not performative ones. Anonymous feedback loops, structured 360-degree reviews, and safe channels for dissent must be put in place to ensure that truth can surface without consequence.

Leaders must also learn to separate identity from ideas. One of the most important shifts a leader can make is understanding that an idea being wrong does not mean they are wrong. Without that separation, every challenge feels personal—and every disagreement becomes a threat.

Organizations must begin rewarding truth, not agreement. Leaders should publicly recognize individuals who challenge constructively and reinforce the value of healthy disagreement when it leads to better outcomes.

Data must also become the arbiter of decisions. The conversation must shift from *What do I think?* to *What does the data tell us?* This removes ego from the equation and brings objectivity into the process.

Finally, leaders must model the behavior themselves. They must be willing to say:

- "I was wrong."
- "That's a better idea."
- "Let's go with your approach."

Because culture does not change through instruction. It changes through example.

If you want truth from your team, you must prove it's safe to give it.

Ego doesn't just block ideas. It blocks reality. When leaders are disconnected from reality, decisions become flawed, opportunities are missed, and performance suffers. And eventually, the organization pays the price.

Like all organizational cancers, ego-driven leadership starts subtly. It hides behind confidence and authority. It spreads quietly through behavior and reshapes how people interact over time. Left untreated, it becomes embedded in the culture. And once it becomes culture, it becomes very difficult to reverse.

The best leaders don't need to be right. They need to get it right.

When ego leads, truth disappears.

Great leaders don't win arguments. They create environments where the best ideas win.

MISALIGNED INCENTIVES

Every organization has a compensation plan. Every team has goals. Every individual is measured. And whether leaders realize it or not, those systems shape behavior more powerfully than any mission statement ever will. Organizations love to say things like, "We are one team," "We prioritize the customer," and "We value collaboration." Those are good words. They sound right. They look good on walls, in presentations, and in leadership meetings.

But the real question is much simpler: **What do you actually reward?**

Because people do not consistently do what you say. They do what you incentivize. That is not cynicism. It is human nature. Incentives create direction. They communicate what matters. They teach people where to focus, what to protect, and what success really looks like inside the system.

As Peter Drucker taught, "People in any organization are always attached to the obsolete, the things that should have worked but did not, the things that once were productive and no longer are."

Misaligned incentives often survive for exactly that reason. They may have made sense at one point, or at least appeared logical, but they no longer match the organization's reality. And when incentives are not aligned with reality, they do not drive performance. They distort it.

I stepped into an organization that had just rebuilt its entire sales team. They were entering a new market, selling a new technology, and trying to gain traction in a space where relationships, trust, and time mattered. There was just one problem: They did not yet have much of a sales funnel.

That alone would have been challenging enough. But the average sales cycle for the product was also long, roughly twelve to eighteen months.

Leadership had implemented what they believed was a logical compensation plan. The structure was straightforward: a base salary with commission paid upon implementation. On paper, that made sense. Commission would be earned when revenue was realized. Leadership believed this would encourage the team to close the right business.

The problem was that the structure was severely misaligned with the reality of the market, the maturity of the funnel, and the financial realities of the people expected to perform inside it.

The sales team quickly realized something leadership had not fully accounted for. They would need to survive almost entirely on salary while waiting a year or more for commissions to materialize. In theory, the commission opportunity looked attractive. In practice, it was too far away to influence daily motivation or financial stability.

The result was predictable.

Not because people were lazy.
Not because they didn't care.
But because the system was asking human beings to operate against their own economic reality.

People began to feel trapped. Financial pressure rose. Motivation weakened. Turnover increased. Morale dropped. The sales process slowed, and the funnel stagnated before it ever had a chance to mature. The system did not motivate performance. It discouraged it.

Over time, the damage became clear:

- Pipeline growth stalled.
- New opportunities were limited.
- Revenue lagged.
- The team lacked urgency and direction.

There was real talent on the team. There was market opportunity. There was even a product worth selling. But the system prevented that potential from being realized.

The problem wasn't the people. It was what the system was rewarding—and what it wasn't.

We made the decision to realign the system. Not with words. Not with motivational speeches. Not with another meeting about culture. With incentives. We introduced a guaranteed commission structure and added quarterly MBO bonuses tied directly to the activities the organization actually needed in order to grow. Those incentives were aligned with what would build momentum in a long sales cycle, including:

- new leads added;
- demos performed;
- funnel expansion; and
- quotes and contracts sent.

This shifted the system from rewarding only distant outcomes to rewarding the behaviors that would create those outcomes. And once that alignment happened, the organization began to move.

The change was noticeable almost immediately. The funnel began to grow. Activity increased. Deals progressed. Contracts moved. Momentum returned. Then came the larger results. Revenue increased. New logos were added. Market share expanded. A strong client referral network began to build.

The people did not change. The system did. And when the system aligned, the organization accelerated.

Misaligned incentives strike at the core of alignment and execution. Within the C.U.R.E.S. framework, they directly damage Unity and Execution.

Unity breaks because teams and individuals begin optimizing for different definitions of success. Instead of working together toward shared outcomes, they protect their own metrics and pursue what benefits them most personally.

Execution breaks because priorities no longer match outcomes. People may be active, busy, and even productive by one measurement, while the organization as a whole falls further behind.

From a **BROT** perspective, trust also begins to erode. People start to question motives. They begin to wonder: *Is this helping the organization, or just helping them?*

And once that question enters the culture, collaboration becomes much harder to sustain.

Severity: High (Systemic Cancer)

This is a high-severity cancer because it is systemic. It is not simply a leadership habit or a communication issue. It is embedded directly into how the organization functions.

It is dangerous because:

- it is built into compensation;
- it reinforces itself daily; and
- it impacts behavior at every level.

When incentives are misaligned, the organization is effectively paying people to create friction.

You can't out-coach a broken incentive system.

Treatment Plan (C.U.R.E.S.)

Misaligned incentives cannot be fixed with messaging alone. They must be fixed through system design.

The first step is aligning goals across teams. Shared KPIs must be created so departments are not pulling in different directions. Success has to be defined at the organizational level, not just at the individual or departmental level.

Compensation structures must also be redesigned to reward the behaviors that actually drive long-term outcomes. Incentives must reflect reality—cycle time, market maturity, collaboration needs, and strategic priorities.

Conflicting metrics must be removed. No team should be rewarded for behavior that harms another team or weakens the organization overall. When one group wins at another's expense, the system is already broken.

Shared wins must be created intentionally. Collaboration should not be a nice idea; it should be rewarded. Team contributions, cross-functional support, and behaviors that strengthen the whole organization must be recognized and reinforced.

Finally, leadership must consistently communicate and model the right philosophy: We win together, or we don't win at all.

If your teams are competing internally, your system is broken.

Misaligned incentives do not just create inefficiency. They create conflict by design. And when conflict is built into the system, no amount of culture work can fully overcome it. Leaders can preach teamwork. They can talk about unity. They can encourage collaboration. But if the system rewards the opposite, the system will win.

Like all organizational cancers, this one starts small. It hides behind performance language. It spreads through systems. It reshapes behavior over time. And left untreated, it becomes normal. It becomes how the organization operates. That is what makes it so dangerous. Alignment is not something you say. It is something you design.

People don't do what you say. They do what you reward.

OVERCOMPLEXITY CANCER

Not all problems in organizations come from what's missing. Some of the most damaging issues come from having too much.

Too many tools. Too many processes. Too many priorities. Too many steps. Too many systems.

What often begins as an effort to improve, to add structure, to increase control, or to create better outcomes slowly transforms into something far more dangerous. It becomes complexity.

At first, complexity feels productive. It looks like progress. More systems are put into place, more processes are defined, and more layers are added to ensure quality and consistency. But over time, those same additions begin to create friction instead of clarity.

As Leonardo da Vinci once said, "Simplicity is the ultimate sophistication."

And yet, simplicity is rarely what organizations choose.

I worked with an organization that believed they had built the perfect system for managing product enhancements and feedback. Their intention was strong. They wanted to create a centralized way for both clients and employees to submit ideas, track requests, and ensure that the best insights were captured and prioritized.

On paper, it was a great idea.

But in reality, it became a perfect example of overcomplexity.

The system required extensive input. It asked too many questions, required too much detail, and took far too long to complete. What should have been a simple submission process felt more like filling out a twelve-page application.

Clients didn't want complexity. They wanted a quick, easy way to share their ideas and suggestions. Employees didn't want complexity either. They wanted a streamlined way to capture what they were hearing in the market, from sales conversations, and from real-world experience. They also wanted visibility. They wanted to know what happened after they submitted their ideas.

Instead, they encountered friction. The process was slow, the system was cumbersome, and there was no feedback loop. Suggestions seemed to disappear into a black hole.

When systems become too complex, people don't push through them. They work around them, or they abandon them entirely.

That's exactly what happened.

People stopped using the system. Many never submitted a second idea after struggling through the first. Some chose not to engage at all. The very system designed to increase innovation ended up suppressing it.

Feedback slowed. Insight disappeared. Opportunities were missed.

And the most dangerous part? Leadership believed the system was working.

Over time, the impact of overcomplexity becomes undeniable. Execution slows because every task requires more effort than it should. Valuable insights are lost because the barriers to sharing them are too high. Employees disengage because the systems meant to help them actually make their jobs harder. Clients feel unheard because their input isn't easily captured or acted upon.

Innovation declines—not because people lack ideas, but because the system makes it too difficult to contribute them.

As Albert Einstein once said, "Any intelligent fool can make things bigger and more complex. It takes a touch of genius, and a lot of courage, to move in the opposite direction."

Overcomplexity is rarely intentional. It's the result of good intentions layered on top of each other without discipline.

Overcomplexity directly attacks two critical elements of the C.U.R.E.S. framework: Clarity and Execution.

Clarity is lost when there are too many priorities, too many paths, and too many competing signals. People no longer know what matters most, and when everything feels important, nothing truly is.

Execution slows because every action requires navigating unnecessary steps, redundant tools, or unclear processes. What should be simple becomes difficult, and what should be fast becomes slow.

While overcomplexity may not immediately destroy trust, it erodes confidence in systems. People begin to feel that the organization's processes are working against them rather than for them.

Severity: Medium (Creeping Cancer)

Overcomplexity is not a fast-moving cancer. It doesn't explode overnight. It builds gradually, layer by layer, process by process, tool by tool.

Because of this, it is often overlooked. But over time, it becomes suffocating.

Everything feels harder than it should. Progress slows. Energy drains. Frustration increases.

Complexity doesn't break organizations overnight; it suffocates them over time.

Treatment Plan (C.U.R.E.S.)

The solution to overcomplexity is not adding more. It is removing what doesn't matter.

Organizations must develop the discipline to simplify.

This begins with reducing priorities. Most organizations try to do too much at once. By narrowing focus to three to five true priorities, clarity returns and execution accelerates.

Workflows must also be simplified. Every step should be evaluated with a simple question: "Does this add value?" If it doesn't, it should be removed. The goal is not to create perfect processes, but to create usable ones.

Redundant tools should be eliminated. Many organizations unknowingly create complexity through overlapping technologies that perform similar functions. Consolidation reduces confusion and increases adoption.

Finally, processes must be standardized. Consistency creates predictability, and predictability enables execution at scale.

If it feels complicated, it probably is. Overcomplexity doesn't just slow execution. It hides truth. When systems are too complex, people disengage. They stop participating fully. Problems go unnoticed because the signals are buried. Systems go unused because they are too difficult to navigate. What leaders believe is control is often just confusion in disguise.

Like all organizational cancers, overcomplexity begins with good intentions. It grows quietly, spreads through systems, and reshapes behavior over time. Left untreated, it becomes the operating model.

The best organizations are not the most complex. They are those that are the clearest.

Complexity is the silent killer of execution.

TECHNOLOGY ILLUSION CANCER

Technology is one of the most powerful enablers in modern organizations. It promises efficiency, visibility, automation, and growth. Because of that, it has also become one of the most misunderstood elements of organizational success. Many organizations fall into the same belief: "If we just get the right tool, everything will improve."

A better CRM. A better EMR. A better platform.

On the surface, that thinking makes sense. Technology has transformed industries and created incredible advantages for those who use it well. But over time, this belief creates a dangerous illusion—that technology alone will fix what are fundamentally people, process, or alignment problems.

As Peter Drucker once said, "There is nothing so useless as doing efficiently that which should not be done at all."

Technology doesn't solve problems. It amplifies them.

I worked with an organization that was growing and performing well. They had momentum, a strong product, and an expanding team. Naturally, they wanted to accelerate sales growth, so they made a logical move: They hired additional sales professionals.

As the team grew, a new challenge quickly surfaced. These individuals were struggling to keep track of their activities, opportunities, follow-ups, and overall pipeline. There was a lack of structure, and it was becoming increasingly difficult to maintain visibility into what was happening across the sales organization.

Leadership identified what they believed was the solution.

"We need the best CRM on the market."

What followed was a significant investment of time and energy into selecting the right platform. They evaluated options, compared features, and ultimately chose what they believed would solve their problems. Once the purchase was made, there was a sense of confidence, almost relief, that the issue had been addressed.

But in reality, the real work had not yet begun. Very little time was spent on what truly determines success with any technology system:

- How it would be used
- How it aligned with sales goals
- What data actually mattered
- How workflows would function
- How the team would be trained

The system was implemented, but it was never truly integrated into how the organization operated. The sales team was left trying to figure it out on their own. And, as often happens, they adapted—not in the way leadership intended, but in the way that allowed them to survive.

They began entering data—not to create clarity or improve performance, but simply to show activity. Fields were filled out inconsistently. Information was incomplete or misaligned. The system became a place to record motion, not to drive meaningful insight. Instead of empowering the team, it overwhelmed them. Instead of creating visibility, it created noise.

Over time, the consequences became clear:

- The sales team felt burdened by the tool.
- Management lacked reliable data.

- Decision-making suffered.
- Pipeline visibility was distorted.
- ROI from the investment never materialized.

Because with technology, and especially systems like CRMs, if you put bad data in, you get bad data out.

The issue was never the tool itself. It was the assumption that the tool would fix the problem. Technology does not create discipline. It does not create clarity. It does not create alignment. It only enhances what already exists.

As W. Edwards Deming taught, "A bad system will beat a good person every time."

This doesn't mean that systems are more important than people. It means that even the most capable, hardworking individuals cannot succeed inside a broken system. And in many organizations, technology becomes that system. When a tool is not aligned with how work actually gets done, when teams are not properly trained, and when there is no clarity around what success looks like, the technology itself becomes the problem. Instead of enabling performance, it restricts it. Instead of creating clarity, it creates confusion. The technology will not solve those problems. It will magnify them.

Even great people can't win inside a broken system. And technology without alignment becomes a broken system fast.

Technology Illusion Cancer directly impacts both Readiness and Execution within the C.U.R.E.S. framework.

Readiness is compromised because the organization is not truly prepared to adopt or utilize the tool effectively. There is a gap between what the system is capable of and what the organization is ready to do with it.

Execution breaks down because workflows are unclear, data is unreliable, and actions become inconsistent. Instead of accelerating performance, the system slows it down.

Over time, this also impacts trust. Teams begin to lose confidence in the systems they are required to use, and leadership decisions tied to those systems start to feel disconnected from reality.

Severity: Medium (Expensive Cancer)

This is a medium-severity cancer, but it carries a high cost.

It doesn't typically destroy an organization overnight, but it quietly drains resources, time, and energy. Organizations invest heavily in tools that never deliver their full value. Teams spend hours working within systems that don't help them perform better. Opportunities are missed, and frustration builds.

Perhaps most dangerous of all is the illusion that progress has been made.

The organization believes it has solved the problem, when in reality, it has only added another layer to it. The illusion of progress is often more dangerous than no progress at all.

Treatment Plan (C.U.R.E.S.)

The solution to Technology Illusion Cancer is not better technology. It is better alignment, better adoption, and better intentional use. Organizations must shift their mindset from focusing on the purchase of tools to focusing on the performance those tools are meant to enable. Technology should follow process, not replace it.

This means taking the time to define workflows before implementation. It means clearly identifying what data matters and why. It means training teams so they understand not just how to use the system, but how it helps them succeed.

It also requires ongoing measurement. Leaders must evaluate whether the technology is being used effectively and whether it is delivering meaningful results. Adoption and ROI must be actively managed, not assumed.

Don't ask if you bought the right tool. Ask if your team is using it the right way.

Technology doesn't fix broken systems. It exposes them. If processes are unclear, if goals are misaligned, or if teams are not equipped to execute, technology will not solve those issues. It will simply make them more visible, and often more frustrating.

Like all organizational cancers, Technology Illusion Cancer begins with good intentions. It grows quietly, spreads through systems, and reshapes behavior over time.

Left untreated, it becomes embedded in how the organization operates, creating inefficiency, frustration, and lost potential.

The best organizations do not rely on technology to solve their problems. They use technology to accelerate what already works.

Technology doesn't fix broken systems; it exposes them.

INITIATIVE OVERLOAD/CHANGE SATURATION

Most organizations don't suffer from a lack of ideas. They suffer from too many. New initiatives are introduced with the best of intentions. New strategies are launched to drive growth. New systems are implemented to improve performance. New priorities are communicated to elevate results.

Individually, each initiative makes sense. Each one is logical. Each one is introduced with energy, optimism, and a belief that it will move the organization forward. But collectively, something very different begins to happen. Instead of progress, organizations experience fragmentation. Instead of alignment, they create confusion. Instead of momentum, they create motion without direction.

As Stephen Covey wisely stated, "The main thing is to keep the main thing the main thing."

The challenge is that in many organizations, there is no longer a clear "main thing." There are too many things competing for attention, resources, and execution. And when everything feels important, nothing truly is.

I once worked with an organization that had everything going for it. Strong leadership, talented people, a growing market, and a genuine desire to accelerate performance. They weren't lacking vision. In fact, they had an abundance of it. At the beginning of the year, leadership unveiled what they called a "transformational roadmap." It was ambitious, comprehensive, and designed to drive significant growth.

The roadmap included:

- a new CRM rollout;
- a complete rebrand;

- a pricing strategy overhaul;
- a new sales methodology;
- territory restructuring;
- a marketing automation platform;
- a leadership-development initiative; and
- multiple strategic growth programs.

On paper, it looked impressive. It signaled innovation, forward thinking, and a commitment to improvement. But inside the organization, it created something very different.

At first, the energy was high. Teams were engaged. Meetings were full. Calendars were packed. There was a sense that something big was happening. Everyone was busy. But within a few months, that energy began to shift.

The organization didn't slow down. In fact, it felt busier than ever. But it stopped moving forward.

People began asking questions they couldn't clearly answer:

- "Which initiative matters most?"
- "What should I prioritize today?"
- "Is this still a focus, or has leadership already moved on?"

The answers varied, depending on who you asked. And when clarity disappears, people default to self-prioritization. Some focused on the CRM rollout. Others leaned into the new sales methodology. Some tried to support everything. Many simply focused on surviving their day-to-day responsibilities.

Alignment quietly disappeared. And in its place, activity without progress took over.

Over time, the consequences became impossible to ignore:

- Teams became overwhelmed.
- Priorities became unclear.
- Execution slowed across the board.
- Initiatives stalled before completion.
- Employees disengaged and burned out.

And perhaps most damaging of all, nothing actually got finished.

The problem wasn't a lack of effort. It was a lack of focus.

As Greg McKeown, author of *Essentialism*, explains, "If you don't prioritize your life, someone else will."

In organizations, if you don't prioritize your initiatives, everything competes for attention—and nothing gets the focus it deserves.

Initiative Overload directly impacts both Readiness and Sustainability within the C.U.R.E.S. framework.

Readiness breaks down because the organization exceeds its capacity for change. Even the most capable teams cannot absorb continuous, overlapping transformation without losing effectiveness.

Sustainability becomes nearly impossible because initiatives are never given the time or reinforcement needed to take hold. Change is introduced but not stabilized. Effort is applied but not sustained.

This creates a repeating cycle: Start strong. Lose focus. Move on. Repeat. And with each cycle, confidence declines—not just in leadership, but in the organization's ability to execute meaningful change.

Severity: High (Burnout Accelerator)

This is a high-severity cancer—not because of any single initiative, but because of the accumulation of them. It drains energy. It erodes focus. It weakens clarity. It accelerates burnout. And it does so faster than most leaders realize.

You don't fail because you do too little. You fail because you try to do too much at once.

Treatment Plan (C.U.R.E.S.)

The solution to initiative overload is not better execution—it is better prioritization. Organizations must develop the discipline to do less, but do it exceptionally well. This begins by limiting active initiatives. Focus must be narrowed intentionally. Not ten priorities. Not even seven. Three to five at most.

Change must also be sequenced. Not everything should happen at once. Initiatives should be introduced in a way that allows the organization to absorb, adapt, and stabilize before introducing the next wave of change.

Leaders must also consider capacity. It is not enough to ask, "Is this important?" The more important question is, "Do we have the capacity to do this well right now?"

Finally, reinforcement must become part of the system. Launching an initiative is only the beginning. It must be supported, measured, and sustained until it becomes part of how the organization operates.

If everything is important, nothing is.

Initiative overload doesn't feel like failure. It feels like progress. That's what makes it so dangerous. Meetings increase. Communication increases. Activity increases. But results do not. Because progress is not defined by how much you start. It is defined by what you finish—and sustain.

Like all organizational cancers, initiative overload begins with good intentions. It grows through leadership decisions, spreads across teams, and reshapes behavior over time. Left untreated, it becomes the culture—a culture of constant change without meaningful progress.

The most successful organizations are not the ones that do the most. They are the ones that focus on what matters most—and execute it exceptionally well.

When everything is a priority, nothing gets done.

LACK OF HONEST SELF-ASSESSMENT

When Organizations Stop Telling Themselves the Truth

Some organizational cancers are loud. Others are subtle. This one is dangerous because it hides in plain sight.

It doesn't look like dysfunction. It often presents itself as confidence, stability, and even success. Organizations convince themselves that things are fine, that issues are small, or that challenges can be addressed later. Over time, this mindset quietly replaces truth with comfort.

And slowly, almost without realizing it, they stop asking the most important question:

"How are we really doing?"

As Peter Drucker famously said, "What gets measured gets managed."

But the inverse is just as true, and far more dangerous.

What doesn't get measured gets ignored.

Through years of consulting, coaching, and leading individuals, I've learned something simple, but incredibly powerful: Growth requires evaluation.

I tell people all the time: "I'm great at ESPN, but terrible at ESP."

I can analyze performance. I can break down what happened. I can look at results and understand patterns. But I can't read minds. I can't assume. I can't guess. And neither can any organization.

If you don't measure it…

If you don't evaluate it...
If you don't ask the hard questions...

You don't actually know.

During the international portion of my MBA program, I had the opportunity to spend time with the CEO of a German company called Veit, an iron and pressing organization. In one conversation, he shared a principle that has stayed with me ever since:

"Never go to bed without learning at least one new item."

At first, it sounds simple. But it's much deeper than that. It's about discipline. It's about reflection. It's about forcing yourself to evaluate the day before you move on from it. At the end of each day, you ask:

"What is one new thing I learned today?"

And if you don't have an answer, you don't accept it. You get out of bed, open a book, and learn something.

Because growth isn't accidental. It's intentional.

When individuals, and organizations stop evaluating honestly, they don't stop moving. They just start drifting.

Without honest self-assessment, problems don't disappear. They simply go unnoticed. Patterns remain unchallenged. Assumptions replace facts. And over time, small issues compound into much larger ones.

Instead of truth, organizations begin to operate on comfort. Instead of clarity, they rely on assumptions. Instead of growth, they experience stagnation.

The absence of honest self-assessment leads to:

- late detection of problems;
- compounding issues over time;
- missed opportunities for improvement;
- leadership blind spots; and
- slower organizational growth.

And perhaps most dangerous of all: A false sense of confidence.

The greatest risk isn't what you know is broken—it's what you think is working, but isn't.

This cancer strikes at the foundation of awareness and preparedness.

It distorts Clarity by creating decisions based on incomplete or inaccurate understanding. Leaders believe they see the full picture, when in reality, they are operating with *Blind Spots.*

It weakens Readiness because the organization is preparing for a version of reality that doesn't actually exist. When truth is unclear, preparation is flawed.

Over time, this can also erode trust. When outcomes don't match expectations, teams begin to lose confidence in leadership direction—not because of intent, but because of a lack of visibility.

Severity: High (Hidden Cancer)

This is a hidden cancer.

It doesn't create immediate pain. It creates delayed consequences. Because of that, it often goes untreated longer than any other cancer.

What makes it especially dangerous is not what it does quickly, but what it allows to happen slowly.

What you don't examine… eventually controls you.

Treatment Plan (C.U.R.E.S.)

The cure is not complicated, but it requires discipline and honesty.

Organizations must build systems that create visibility and force truth to the surface. This is where your C.U.R.E.S. diagnostic scorecards and dashboards become essential. They remove guesswork and replace it with measurable reality across Clarity, Unity, Readiness, Execution, and Sustainability.

Data must be visible. Trends must be reviewed consistently. Leadership must commit to regular business reviews—not just when things go wrong, but as a standard operating rhythm.

Most importantly, organizations must make a conscious decision to choose truth over comfort.

The same principle that applies to individuals applies to organizations.

You must ask, consistently and honestly:

- What is going well?
- What is not going well?
- What needs to change?
- What needs to continue?

And then, you must be willing to accept the answers.

Because when you do this consistently, improvement becomes inevitable. Growth becomes natural. Progress becomes sustainable.

Like all organizational cancers, this one starts small. It hides behind confidence. It spreads quietly and limits potential over time.

But unlike many others, it prevents you from even seeing the problem. And if you can't see it, you can't treat it.

Growth is not a mystery. It is the result of awareness. Organizations don't improve because they want to. They improve because they **measure, evaluate, and adjust.**

You can't cure what you refuse to diagnose.

C.U.R.E.S. Organizational Health Scorecard

Rate each statement from 1 to 5 (1 = Strongly Disagree, 5 = Strongly Agree)

#	CLARITY	Score (1-5)
1.	Our organization has a clearly defined and communicated strategy	
2.	Leadership is aligned on top priorities	
3.	Every department understands how their work ties to company goals	
4.	Roles and responsibilities are clearly defined	
5.	Decision-making authority is clearly established	
6.	We have a small number of prioritized KPIs that drive behavior	
7.	Our technology has clearly defined use-cases and success metrics	
8.	Teams rarely feel confused about what matters most	
	Clarity Subtotal	
#	**UNITY**	**Score (1-5)**
1.	Leadership operates as a unified team (not individual agendas)	
2.	Departments collaborate effectively across functions	
3.	Incentives are aligned across teams (not competing)	
4.	Communication between teams is consistent and productive	
5.	Issues are addressed directly, not avoided or escalated late	
6.	There is trust between leadership and frontline staff	
7.	Meetings drive alignment, not confusion	
8.	We solve problems cross-functionally, not in silos	
	Unity Subtotal	
#	**READINESS**	**Score (1-5)**
1.	Our organization is prepared for the level of growth we are pursuing	
2.	We do not implement change faster than we can absorb it	
3.	Our processes are documented and repeatable	
4.	New hires are onboarded effectively and consistently	
5.	We have the right talent in the right roles	
6.	Our technology supports our workflows (not fights them)	
7.	Teams are trained before new systems/processes are rolled out	
8.	We assess readiness before launching major initiatives	
	Readiness Subtotal	

#	EXECUTION	Score (1-5)
1.	We consistently execute our top priorities	
2.	Accountability is clear and enforced	
3.	Projects are completed on time and as planned	
4.	Workflows are efficient and consistently followed	
5.	Technology is fully utilized in day-to-day operations	
6.	We have regular performance tracking and review cadence	
7.	Leaders follow through on commitments	
8.	We avoid constant firefighting and reactive work	
	Execution Subtotal	
#	**SUSTAINABILITY**	**Score (1-5)**
1.	Improvements we make tend to stick long-term	
2.	We have systems to monitor performance continuously	
3.	Leadership behaviors reinforce desired culture	
4.	We proactively identify risks before they become problems	
5.	We use dashboards or scorecards to track organizational health	
6.	Teams continuously improve processes (not just fix problems)	
7.	We do not constantly restart initiatives from scratch	
8.	We have a clear governance model for decision-making	
	Sustainability Subtotal	
	Total Score	

C.U.R.E.S. Scoring Guide
Each section has 8 questions scored 1–5. Section subtotals range: 8 to 40
Suggested Section Subtotal Interpretation / Suggested Total Score Interpretation
32–40 = STRONG = 160-200
24–31 = AT RISK = 120-159
8–23 = CRITICAL GAP = 40-119

ABOUT THE AUTHOR

Christopher Taylor is a business and leadership consultant, speaker, and author of *The Corporate Cure*, a leadership framework designed to help organizations diagnose and eliminate the root causes of organizational breakdown. As the Founder and CEO of Taylor'd Growth, Chris works with leadership teams and organizations to improve alignment, execution, operational performance, and sustainable growth.

With more than 30 years of executive leadership, business development, sales, operational, and consulting experience across multiple industries, Chris brings a practical, results-driven approach to helping organizations simplify complexity, strengthen culture, optimize performance, and drive measurable outcomes. His expertise spans leadership development, organizational growth, sales transformation, DISC analysis, technology optimization, executive strategy, and organizational consulting.

Chris is widely recognized for his deep expertise in healthcare and the Care-at-Home industry, including home health, hospice, private duty, palliative care, and healthcare technology. Throughout his career, he has worked with providers, hospitals, vendors, executive teams, and organizations nationwide to strengthen leadership, optimize operations, improve technology utilization, and accelerate growth.

Prior to founding Taylor'd Growth, Chris served in executive leadership roles, including Chief Revenue Officer (CRO), EVP of Sales, and SVP of Partnerships for nationally recognized organizations, where he built high-performing teams, developed strategic partnerships, and led transformational growth initiatives. A graduate of the BYU Marriott School of Management, Chris earned his MBA as the top graduate in his class, specializing in organizational behavior and leadership development. He is known for his ability to connect strategy with execution and help organizations build healthier, more aligned, and sustainable cultures.

But beyond business and leadership, Chris considers his greatest success to be his family. He and his wife Elise are blessed with eight children and thirteen grandchildren, who bring purpose, perspective, and tremendous joy to his life. When he isn't consulting, speaking, or writing, Chris enjoys staying active through pickleball, scuba diving, traveling, and taking in Broadway musicals. He believes leadership is ultimately about people, relationships, and making a positive impact—and that philosophy guides both his work and his life.

WHAT WE CAN DO FOR YOU

Beyond The Book. Into Transformation.

How Taylor'd Growth Helps Organizations Align, Execute, and Sustain Results

Reading *The Corporate Cure* is the beginning. Transformation happens when ideas are put into action with clarity, accountability, and execution. Through Taylor'd Growth, Chris Taylor and his team work directly with organizations to diagnose challenges, align leadership, strengthen culture, optimize performance, and drive measurable results.

With more than 30 years of executive leadership, operational, sales, and consulting experience across multiple industries, Chris brings real-world perspective—not just theory. Every engagement is practical, customized, and focused on helping organizations move from reactive to proactive.

C.U.R.E.S. Coaching

The C.U.R.E.S. Framework was designed to help organizations create sustainable transformation through Clarity, Unity, Readiness, Execution, and Sustainability. Through customized coaching engagements, Taylor'd Growth helps leadership teams diagnose breakdowns, identify root causes, create strategic alignment, and build actionable roadmaps that improve culture, execution, accountability, and long-term organizational health.

Whether your organization is struggling with growth, communication, alignment, leadership challenges, or operational inefficiencies, C.U.R.E.S. Coaching provides a proven framework to help you move forward with confidence and purpose.

BROT—Trust and Team Building

Strong organizations are built on trust. Weak trust creates friction, silos, politics, disengagement, and poor execution. The BROT Framework (Building Relationships of Trust) helps organizations strengthen transparency, communication, reliability, and accountability at every level of the business.

Taylor'd Growth works with executive teams, departments, and organizations to assess trust gaps, improve collaboration, strengthen communication, and create cultures where people feel connected, valued, aligned, and accountable. Because when trust improves, performance follows.

Keynote Speaking and Executive Retreats

Chris Taylor delivers high-impact keynote presentations and executive retreats designed to challenge thinking, inspire action, and create meaningful organizational transformation. Combining real-world executive experience, engaging storytelling, practical frameworks, and interactive leadership concepts, Chris helps leaders and teams rethink culture, leadership, trust, execution, and organizational performance.

From conference stages to private executive retreats, these experiences are designed to create clarity, alignment, and momentum that organizations can immediately apply to their business.

Sales Training—Tactical and Strategic

Most organizations do not have a sales problem—they have a strategy, execution, and consistency problem. Taylor'd Growth provides customized sales training designed to strengthen both tactical selling skills and long-term strategic growth initiatives.

With decades of executive sales leadership experience, Chris helps organizations improve sales structure, leadership alignment, accountability, messaging, relationship development, pipeline management, and growth strategy. Whether building a new sales culture or optimizing an existing team, the goal is simple: create sustainable sales performance that drives measurable outcomes.

DISC Analysis and Team Dynamics

Every organization communicates—but not every organization communicates effectively. DISC assessments and training help individuals and teams better understand communication styles, motivations, strengths, *Blind Spots*, and interpersonal dynamics.

Taylor'd Growth uses DISC as a practical leadership and team-development tool to improve communication, reduce conflict, strengthen collaboration, and help leaders better connect with employees, customers, and teams. When people understand how to communicate with one another more effectively, trust, engagement, and performance improve dramatically.

Leadership Mentoring

Leadership is not about titles—it is about influence, accountability, vision, and the ability to elevate others. Through executive mentoring and leadership coaching, Chris works one-on-one with leaders to help them strengthen decision-making, communication, execution, strategic thinking, team development, and leadership confidence.

Drawing from more than three decades of executive leadership experience, Chris helps leaders navigate growth, complexity, culture challenges, organizational change, and career development while building leadership habits that create long-term impact.

Technology Selection and Optimization Consulting

Organizations invest millions into technology—but many never fully utilize the systems they already own. Taylor'd Growth helps organizations evaluate, optimize, select, and implement technology solutions that improve operational efficiency, communication, compliance, execution, and financial performance.

From technology audits and workflow optimization to vendor selection, EMR evaluations, process redesign, and strategic technology consulting, Taylor'd Growth helps organizations ensure their technology investments are aligned with outcomes—not just features. Because technology only creates value when it drives results.

Let's Continue the Conversation

If *The Corporate Cure* challenged your thinking, exposed opportunities, or helped you identify areas for growth within your organization, let's talk.

Taylor'd Growth exists to help organizations diagnose what's broken, align what matters, and build what lasts.

TAYLOR'D GROWTH

Diagnose. Align. Heal. Grow.

taylordgrowth.com

Schedule a consultation, leadership workshop, keynote, or organizational assessment today.